ON YOUR MARK, GET SET, GOLD!

**TO GWEN
"THERE'S A GOOD FILM ON TONIGHT . . ."**
SA

**TO MY DEAR LITTLE CHAMPIONS
JULIETTE ET BASILE**
AC

Text copyright © 2020 by Scott Allen
Illustrations copyright © 2020 by Antoine Corbineau
Nosy Crow and its logos are trademarks of Nosy Crow Ltd. Used under license.

First US edition 2020
First published by Nosy Crow (UK) 2020

Library of Congress Catalog Card Number pending
ISBN 978-1-5362-1398-0

20 21 22 23 24 25 WKT 10 9 8 7 6 5 4 3 2 1

Printed in Shenzhen, Guangdong, China

This book was typeset in Aromatica.
The illustrations were created digitally.

Nosy Crow
an imprint of
Candlewick Press
99 Dover Street
Somerville, Massachusetts 02144

www.nosycrow.com
www.candlewick.com

ON YOUR MARK,
GET SET,
GOLD!

AN IRREVERENT GUIDE
TO THE SPORTS OF THE SUMMER GAMES

Scott Allen

illustrated by

Antoine Corbineau

nosy crow

An imprint of Candlewick Press

Contents

Introduction 6

How Did the Olympics Begin? 8

HAVING A BALL

Basketball 10
Soccer 12
Goalball 14
Rugby 16
Handball 18
Field Hockey 20
Boccia 22
Volleyball 24
Baseball and Softball 26

TAKING AIM

Golf 28
Shooting 30
Archery 32

FIGHTING FIT

Boxing 34
Fencing 36
Judo 38
Karate 40
Wrestling 42
Taekwondo 44

SPLASHING AROUND

Aquatics
Swimming 46
Diving 48
Water Polo 50
Artistic Swimming 52
Canoe 54
Surfing 56
Rowing 58
Sailing 60

PUSHING THE LIMITS

Athletics
- Track Events — 62
- Field Events — 64
- Decathlon and Heptathlon — 66

Gymnastics
- Artistic — 68
- Trampoline — 70
- Rhythmic — 71

Sport Climbing — 72
Triathlon — 74
Modern Pentathlon — 75
Weightlifting — 76

MAKING A RACKET

Badminton — 78
Tennis — 80
Table Tennis — 82

RIDING HIGH

Cycling
- Track and Road — 84
- Mountain Bike — 86
- BMX — 87

Equestrian — 88
Skateboarding — 90

What About the Future? — 92

Glossary — 94

Index — 96

INTRODUCTION

Hello and welcome to your funny and fact-filled guide to the Summer Games.
Some sports you might already play, some you will have heard of before but never tried,
and some might be brand new. But remember, with every sport in this guide, you could have
a chance of winning something very special: a gold medal!

But first, becoming a top athlete takes dedication, determination, skill, and a good slice of
old-fashioned luck. Most gold medal winners start their journey when they're still in school,
and some even start while they're in diapers! They face a roller coaster of emotion and physical
torment, but top athletes stay strong, grit their teeth, and battle for glory.

Nobody wins a gold medal without putting in plenty of hard work, so training is essential.
There are lots of different approaches to training, and this guide might give you an edge
against your rivals (or make your dad angry that you've ruined the carpet). In the world of
sports, everyone has to make sacrifices . . . even parents.

We hope that this guide will inspire you to get involved. But what if you're thinking you'll never be good enough to compete at this level? Guess what! You never know until you try. Everybody has the potential to become great at one sport, maybe even two or three. You just have to discover the sport you enjoy the most and train to become more and more skilled at it. You might think you're an average soccer player and you're okay at swimming, but have you ever tried water polo or wrestling? Have you ever climbed to the top of a high diving board and leaped from it or ridden a horse to music? Probably not. However, if you do decide to try something new, you might just discover an amazing hidden talent waiting to be shared with the world.

And even if you don't win a gold medal, you will have gathered some important life skills in your quest. You'll make new friends, become part of a team, get fit and healthy, and, most importantly, have a lot of fun. Many courageous athletes who don't even get close to winning a medal become an inspiration to generations of young athletes around the world. So what are you waiting for?

ON YOUR MARK, GET SET, GOLD!

HOW DID THE GAMES BEGIN?

The first thing to remember is there are two types of Summer Games—the ancient ones and the modern ones—and there was a 1,500-year gap between them. Since 1960, there have also been Paralympic Games, too. Here's a quick guide so you don't get them all muddled up.

Ancient Games

Years active: 776 BCE to 393 CE

Inventor: Ancient Greeks

Host city: Olympia

Competitors: Greek men. Women were only allowed to own and train horses for equestrian events.

Sports included: Running, boxing, wrestling, pentathlon, and equestrian events

Equipment: Not much equipment or even clothes

Prizes: An olive wreath crown made of leaves from Zeus's sacred grove. No prizes for second or third. The best of the best had statues, songs, and stories made up about them.

Top stars:
- **Leonidas of Rhodes** - *Running* - Winner of 12 individual victory wreaths (a record held until 2016)
- **Cynisca of Sparta** - *Equestrian, four-horse chariot* - First female victor at the Olympics
- **Milo of Croton** - *Wrestling* - Six-time victor and known for carrying bulls around on his shoulders and tearing trees apart

Modern Games

Years active: 1896 to present day

Inventor: Baron Pierre de Coubertin, a French aristocrat and academic. He won a gold medal in the 1912 Olympics for a poem!

Host cities: All over the world, although the Olympics has never had an African city as a host

Competitors: Any country with a National Olympic Committee

Sports included: See pages 10–90 to find out.

Equipment: Loads and loads, but a pair of sneakers is probably the most important.

Prizes: A gold, silver, or bronze medal; glory in your country; lots of appearances on TV and sponsorship deals. The best of the best still have statues, songs, and stories made up about them.

Top stars:
- **Michael Phelps** - *USA, Swimming* - 28 medals (23 gold)
- **Larisa Latynina** - *USSR, Gymnastics* - 18 medals (9 gold)
- **Nikolai Andrianov** - *USSR, Gymnastics* - 15 medals (7 gold)

Paralympic Games

Years active: 1960 to present day

Inventor: Dr. Ludwig Guttmann organized the Stoke Mandeville Games for wheelchair athletes, which later became the Paralympic Games. It wasn't called the Paralympics until 1988. *Para* means "beside," showing that the two Games work side by side.

Host city: In the same city as the Olympics

Competitors: Only wheelchair athletes competed until 1976, when it was expanded to include athletes with a much wider range of impairments.

Sports included: Almost the same as the Olympics. There are just two sports that feature only at the Paralympics: goalball and boccia.

Equipment: Depends on the sport, but some Paralympians have specially adapted equipment like running blades.

Prizes: The same as the Olympics. It's all about the medals!

Top stars:
- **Trischa Zorn** - *USA, Swimming* - 55 medals (41 gold)
- **Roberto Marson** - *Italy, Athletics, swimming, and fencing* - 26 medals (16 gold)
- **Heinz Frei** - *Switzerland, Athletics and cycling* - 26 medals (14 gold)

MODERN SUMMER OLYMPICS SO FAR

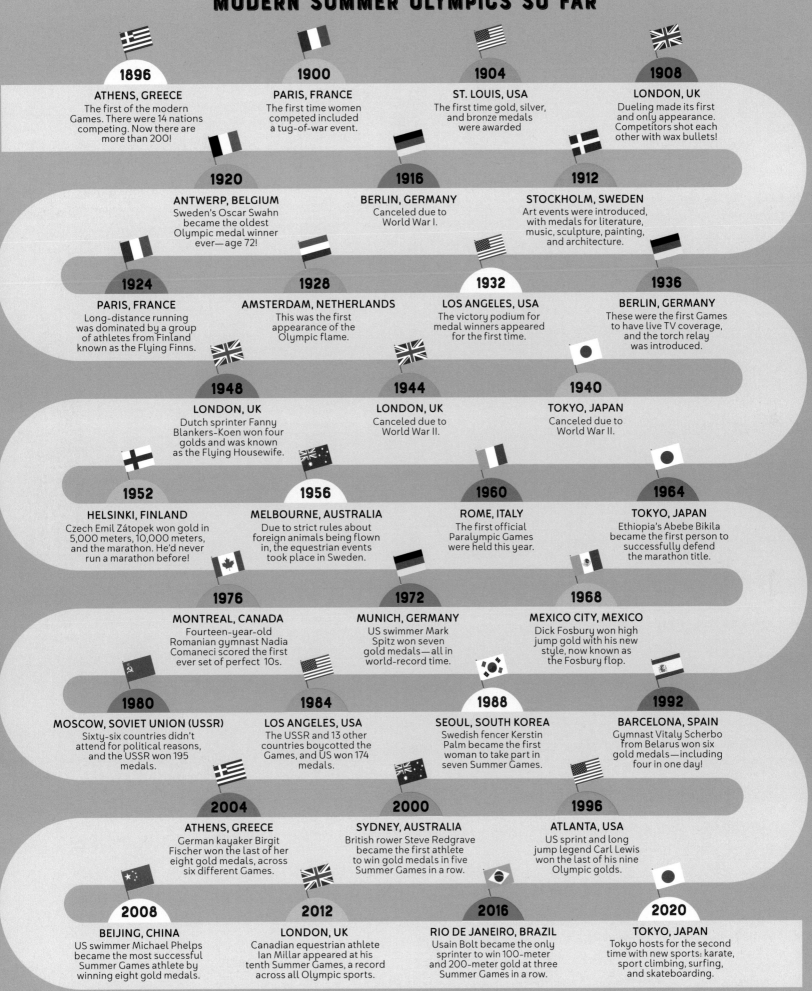

1896 ATHENS, GREECE
The first of the modern Games. There were 14 nations competing. Now there are more than 200!

1900 PARIS, FRANCE
The first time women competed included a tug-of-war event.

1904 ST. LOUIS, USA
The first time gold, silver, and bronze medals were awarded

1908 LONDON, UK
Dueling made its first and only appearance. Competitors shot each other with wax bullets!

1920 ANTWERP, BELGIUM
Sweden's Oscar Swahn became the oldest Olympic medal winner ever—age 72!

1916 BERLIN, GERMANY
Canceled due to World War I.

1912 STOCKHOLM, SWEDEN
Art events were introduced, with medals for literature, music, sculpture, painting, and architecture.

1924 PARIS, FRANCE
Long-distance running was dominated by a group of athletes from Finland known as the Flying Finns.

1928 AMSTERDAM, NETHERLANDS
This was the first appearance of the Olympic flame.

1932 LOS ANGELES, USA
The victory podium for medal winners appeared for the first time.

1936 BERLIN, GERMANY
These were the first Games to have live TV coverage, and the torch relay was introduced.

1948 LONDON, UK
Dutch sprinter Fanny Blankers-Koen won four golds and was known as the Flying Housewife.

1944 LONDON, UK
Canceled due to World War II.

1940 TOKYO, JAPAN
Canceled due to World War II.

1952 HELSINKI, FINLAND
Czech Emil Zátopek won gold in 5,000 meters, 10,000 meters, and the marathon. He'd never run a marathon before!

1956 MELBOURNE, AUSTRALIA
Due to strict rules about foreign animals being flown in, the equestrian events took place in Sweden.

1960 ROME, ITALY
The first official Paralympic Games were held this year.

1964 TOKYO, JAPAN
Ethiopia's Abebe Bikila became the first person to successfully defend the marathon title.

1976 MONTREAL, CANADA
Fourteen-year-old Romanian gymnast Nadia Comaneci scored the first ever set of perfect 10s.

1972 MUNICH, GERMANY
US swimmer Mark Spitz won seven gold medals—all in world-record time.

1968 MEXICO CITY, MEXICO
Dick Fosbury won high jump gold with his new style, now known as the Fosbury flop.

1980 MOSCOW, SOVIET UNION (USSR)
Sixty-six countries didn't attend for political reasons, and the USSR won 195 medals.

1984 LOS ANGELES, USA
The USSR and 13 other countries boycotted the Games, and US won 174 medals.

1988 SEOUL, SOUTH KOREA
Swedish fencer Kerstin Palm became the first woman to take part in seven Summer Games.

1992 BARCELONA, SPAIN
Gymnast Vitaly Scherbo from Belarus won six gold medals—including four in one day!

2004 ATHENS, GREECE
German kayaker Birgit Fischer won the last of her eight gold medals, across six different Games.

2000 SYDNEY, AUSTRALIA
British rower Steve Redgrave became the first athlete to win gold medals in five Summer Games in a row.

1996 ATLANTA, USA
US sprint and long jump legend Carl Lewis won the last of his nine Olympic golds.

2008 BEIJING, CHINA
US swimmer Michael Phelps became the most successful Summer Games athlete by winning eight gold medals.

2012 LONDON, UK
Canadian equestrian athlete Ian Millar appeared at his tenth Summer Games, a record across all Olympic sports.

2016 RIO DE JANEIRO, BRAZIL
Usain Bolt became the only sprinter to win 100-meter and 200-meter gold at three Summer Games in a row.

2020 TOKYO, JAPAN
Tokyo hosts for the second time with new sports: karate, sport climbing, surfing, and skateboarding.

BASKETBALL

WHAT IS IT?

A team sport in which really, really tall people hurl a big orange ball through a hoop hung high in the air

A BIT OF HISTORY

Basketball was invented in 1891, using a peach basket as a hoop, so it's a relatively young sport. It quickly spread through universities across the United States and then around the world and was popular enough by 1936 that it became an Olympic sport that year. Wheelchair basketball has been at the Paralympics since the first Games, in 1960.

The Rules

Two teams of five have to shoot the ball through their opponent's basketball hoop. To move the ball forward, players run while dribbling the ball (bouncing it on the floor) or pass it to one of their teammates. It's two points for baskets thrown from inside the three-point line and three points for those outside. Pushing and shoving the other team isn't allowed; these actions are called fouls. The team with the most points at the end of four quarters wins.

HEADBAND
Basketball is a sweaty sport; these keep you from dripping all over the court.

GOGGLES
If your eyesight isn't good, then these are a must.

A CLOSER LOOK

HOOP
The hoop, also called the rim, is 18 inches (46 centimeters) wide and strong enough for players to hang from after dunks.

SNEAKERS
They support your ankles, and the air-cushioned soles help with higher leaps.

FREE THROW LINE
Players shoot from here after being fouled. These shots are worth one point each.

BASIC TRAINING

Bouncing a ball is a natural thing to do, so now do it lots of times while running. After you've run around a bit, stop and throw the ball at the top of a very high wall. When you're comfortable doing this, add lots of tricks so you look cool.

UPSIDES

It's fast and high scoring. Games never end 0-0. Scores of 98-102 are more likely—that's a lot of baskets. So even if you're not very good, there's a chance you might score. Just chuck the ball up there and see what happens.

DOWNSIDES

Some basketball players will hog the ball, so it can feel like you're spending all your time running up and down the court without ever getting a chance to do more.

BACKBOARD
Always clear, so people sitting behind it still get a good view of the action.

BALL
In the past, balls were heavy and bounced all over the place. Now they're much lighter but still bounce all over the place.

BASKET
This has a hole cut out of the bottom, so isn't really much of a basket.

THE PAINT
If you are attacking, don't hang around in here for more than three seconds or the ball is given to the opposition.

THREE-POINT LINE
Shots from outside this line score three points; shots made from inside the line are worth two points.

SKILLS NEEDED
Anyone can play basketball, but players are known for being tall. The average height for male players is 6 feet 7 inches (202 centimeters). The average height for female players is 6 feet (185 centimeters). So height is a plus, but so are speed, agility, and ball-handling skills.

Height is not important in wheelchair basketball, but you do need good balance, skill, and strong wrists, shoulders, and arms.

INJURIES
With all that twisting, pivoting, and jumping, basketball players get a lot of ankle and foot injuries. That large ball also hurts like crazy if it hits you on the tops of your fingers, so make sure you learn how to catch it properly.

Sound Like a Pro

"ALLEY-OOP"
When a player jumps, catches a pass in midair, and slams the ball into the basket

"DUNK"
To slam the ball into the basket from above the rim

"TRAVELING"
Running with the ball in your hands instead of bouncing it

"BUZZER BEATER"
A shot made in the final second of a game

CHANCE OF BECOMING A CHAMPION

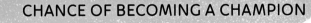

Slim	Okay	Good	Great

Pretty slim. Basketball is one of the most popular sports in the world with more than 20 million people playing in the United States alone. You better start training now.

BEST EVER
Unsurprisingly, the United States has dominated in both men's and women's events. They've won 28 medals, 23 of them gold. Russia is next, with just 12.

SOCCER

WHAT IS IT?

Two teams of 11 try to kick a ball past a goalkeeper into their opponent's net to score a goal. After scoring, they celebrate wildly or do a silly dance.

The Rules

Soccer has lots of rules nowadays, but basically two teams must kick or head the ball into the other team's net. Only the goalkeepers are allowed to touch the ball with their hands, and only in their own area. If you foul your opponents, you may get ejected from the game.

SKILLS NEEDED

All kinds of skills can be applied to being a top soccer player, but not all of them are vital. It helps if goalkeepers are tall and good with their hands. Defenders should be tough and good at tackling and heading. Midfielders should be quick, able to do tricks, and good at passing and tackling. Strikers should be fast and good at shooting.

A BIT OF HISTORY

A version of soccer first began in China back in 300 BCE, and since then various ancient civilizations have played ball games involving their feet. However, it wasn't until the Middle Ages in the UK that soccer began to take off, and proper rules were drawn up in 1863. Soccer first appeared in the Olympics in 1900, but only three teams entered and nobody was awarded a medal.

GOAL
The top rail of the goal is 2.44 meters (8 feet) high, so it's perfect for bored goalkeepers to swing on when action is at the other end of the field.

CAPTAIN'S ARMBAND
The team captain leads the team onto the field, tosses the coin to start, and does most of the shouting at his team and the referee.

A CLOSER LOOK

SOCCER CLEATS
Available in every color of the rainbow, with studs for grip

INJURIES
Soccer players sometimes roll around on the field screaming in pain like they've been hit with an iron bar. Then moments later, they are totally fine. This is known as diving.

BALL
Used to be made out of a pig's bladder or heavy leather, but now it's fake plasticky leather and much lighter.

NET
Stops the ball from flying into the crowd and hitting a spectator in the face.

Slim	Okay	Good	Great

Soccer is the most popular sport in the world.

GOALKEEPER GLOVES
Protect fingers and help keepers get a better grip on the ball.

RED CARD
Get one of these and you are sent off and have to go back to the locker room for a little cry.

REFEREE
The person in charge of the game

UPSIDES
Soccer players are among some of the richest and most famous people in the world.

DOWNSIDES
Being rich and famous sometimes isn't all that it's cracked up to be.

BASIC TRAINING
Get a ball—it doesn't matter how big or small—and practice juggling it using your feet and head. Try to keep it off the floor. Then find a wall and kick the ball at the wall as many times as you can. Pretend you're scoring the winning goal in a final.

Sound Like a Pro

"TIKI-TAKA"
A style of play with short, quick passing and movement

"RABONA"
A kick made by wrapping the kicking foot around the back of the standing leg

"NUTMEG"
A move in which a player dribbles the ball through an opponent's legs and collects it on the other side

"UNDERDOG"
A team that spends the game hiding under a dog—not! It's a team that isn't expected to win.

"ROW Z"
To boot the ball as far away into the crowd as possible to waste time

SHIN GUARDS
Protective covering for shins worn under socks

BEST EVER
The queens of Olympic women's soccer are the USA team, which has won four gold medals and one silver. Hungary's men's team has won three golds, a silver, and a bronze, while Brazil's men's team has the most medals with six, but only one of them is gold.

Goalball

WHAT IS IT?

A team sport in which players roll a hard rubber ball with two bells in it toward a large goal in an attempt to score

A BIT OF HISTORY

Goalball was invented after World War II to help visually impaired soldiers with their recovery. It was so popular that it became a men's Paralympic sport in 1976, and women's in 1984. Goalball is one of only two Paralympic sports that doesn't have a matching sport at the Olympics.

SKILLS NEEDED

To generate power when they roll the ball, many goalball players use a 360-degree turn-and-roll technique. This sometimes causes the ball to bounce slightly, making it harder to stop.

Players need a lot of skill, tactical knowledge, and split-second reactions. There's hardly a moment to take a breather.

A CLOSER LOOK

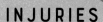

EYESHADES

Goalball is played by athletes who may have varying degrees of visual impairments, so every player wears blackout eyeshades to keep things even. Athletes can't touch their eyeshades without permission from the referee.

INJURIES

Goalball players will use any part of their body to stop the ball from going in the net, so be prepared to get hit in the face by the ball.

The Rules

The aim of goalball is to score as many goals as possible, in two 12-minute halves, by rolling the ball into your opponent's net. The defending team tries to block the ball with their bodies, usually at full stretch. It's like having three goalies.

It's a very fast-flowing game. Each team has three players on court at a time, with three substitutes, and teams have just ten seconds to throw the ball back to the other team. Balls can reach speeds of 50 miles (80 kilometers) per hour! The crowd needs to be totally silent when the ball is in play so the players can hear the ball and each other, but cheering is allowed when a goal is scored.

UPSIDES

There are very few sports exclusively for visually impaired athletes. It's fast moving, and with only three players on each side, you are always in the thick of the action.

DOWNSIDES

You will spend most of the game on the floor. Also, the bigger the crowd, the harder it is to keep them quiet.

A LARGE, LONG GOAL
The goal stretches the whole 9-meter width of the playing area.

HIP PADDING, KNEE AND ELBOW PADS, AND CHEST PROTECTORS
Because athletes spend a lot of time on the court floor

A LARGE RUBBER BALL WITH TWO BELLS IN IT
The sound helps the players follow the ball.

STRING
The court is marked out with string to help players know where they are.

OFFICIALS
There are more officials than players on court: two referees, plus goal judges, timers, and scorers.

Sound Like a Pro

"DISCUS THROW"
A throw in which a player crouches down, rotates 360 degrees, and releases the ball so it bounces near them. Designed to bamboozle the defenders.

"HIGH-ARM DISCUS THROW"
A discus throw with the player staying upright. Even more bamboozling.

"BRAZILIAN SPECIAL"
When a player throws the ball backward between their legs toward the opposing goal.

BEST EVER

Goalball is a very open competition, and no country really dominates the medals. Finland and Denmark are the only countries with two gold medals in the men's event; the USA and Canada each have two golds in the women's competition. The USA has 12 medals in total across both men and women's events.

CHANCE OF BECOMING A CHAMPION

Slim — Okay — Good — Great

If you have a visual impairment, goalball is a great sport to get involved with. Start young, and your chances of making it to this level are greatly increased.

BASIC TRAINING

Tie a scarf over your eyes and get a family member to ring a bell in your house and see if you can find it in a couple of seconds. Avoid having the bell thrown at you, since that might hurt.

RUGBY

WHAT IS IT?

A team sport in which players move an oval ball over the goal line by running with it and passing it sideways or backward

SCRUM CAP
Protects players' ears from injuries, including cauliflower ear

A CLOSER LOOK

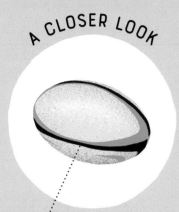

MOUTH GUARD
To prevent players' teeth from getting knocked out

RUGBY BALL
Covered in dimples for good grip so players can pass it with speed and accuracy

CLOSE-FITTING, LIGHTWEIGHT TOPS
Harder to grab than the cotton jerseys players used to wear

SKILLS NEEDED

Rugby players need to be strong, quick, good at ball handling and tackling, and have lots of stamina.

MUD
If you don't like getting muddy, then rugby is not the sport for you.

Sound Like a Pro

"GARRYOWEN" or **"BOMB"**
A high short kick into the air

"BLOOD BIN"
Players who are bleeding have to be subbed out, or sent to "the blood bin."

"HOSPITAL PASS"
A terrible pass, usually made when a player is about to get tackled

STURDY, STUDDED CLEATS
For grip when running or crashing into players on muddy ground

A BIT OF HISTORY

The ancient Roman game *harpastum* and medieval versions of rugby involved carrying the ball. However, it's the story of a schoolboy from Rugby, England, who is said to have invented the game in 1823 by picking up a ball and running with it, that's famous all over the world.

Rugby joined the Summer Games as a 15-player sport in 1900, but then only appeared occasionally after that. The seven-player version of the game made its debut in 2016, and wheelchair rugby, or "murderball," became a Paralympic sport in 2000.

CHANCE OF BECOMING A CHAMPION

Slim | Okay | Good | Great

Rugby's popularity is growing across the world, but it's still only played at a very high standard by a handful of countries such as New Zealand, Australia, South Africa, and the UK.

BASIC TRAINING

Sit on a soccer ball until it's gone into a wonky shape, then pick it up and start bashing into things. Try the sofa cushions first, as most other stuff tends to hurt.

The Rules

This version of rugby is the "sevens" version of the game, rather than the traditional 15-player game. Two teams of seven play seven-minute halves on a full-size rugby field, called a pitch. Players can score a try for five points by placing the ball behind one of the goal lines at either end of the pitch. They can get an extra two points by kicking the ball over the H-shaped posts for a conversion. Three points are gained by a drop goal or a converted penalty — both must go over the posts. Players can carry the ball in their hands but may pass it to another player only by throwing it horizontally or backward.

Wheelchair rugby uses a round ball and is played indoors, with only four players from each mixed-gender team allowed on the court at one time. Games are played in eight-minute quarters. Players who have the ball must pass or bounce it within ten seconds. Tackling may involve touching the ball in another player's possession or smashing one's wheelchair into the ball carrier's chair. This can create havoc, with wheelchairs tipping up all over the court.

INJURIES

Rugby is a full-contact sport, so injuries are numerous and varied. Forwards get injured the most because they're involved in lots of tackles. Strains, bruises, fractures, and broken bones are common.

UPSIDES

Charging your way downfield with the ball, riding tackles, and bashing into people to score a try is great fun.

DOWNSIDES

If you're not quick enough, you can get bashed around a lot.

Wheelchair Rugby

GLOVES WITH ADDED STICKY GRIP
In wheelchair rugby, gloves are an important part of a player's equipment.

BALL
The ball used in wheelchair rugby is a bit like a volleyball with a special surface to add grip.

BEST EVER

Fiji claimed the first rugby sevens men's gold. Australia won the first women's sevens gold. The United States has the most wheelchair rugby medals, with six total, three of them gold.

COMPETITIVE WHEELCHAIR
There are two types: one for attacking players and one for defense.

HANDBALL

WHAT IS IT?

A ball sport for giants, where teams of seven try to score as many goals as possible by throwing the ball into a large net with one hand. It's super-fast.

GOAL
The goal is about 2 meters (8 feet) high. Its posts and crossbar are painted in red and white stripes.

The Rules

Players cannot take more than three steps without dribbling and cannot hold the ball for more than three seconds before passing, shooting, or dribbling. Shots on goal must be from outside the goal area, although attacking players can go in the area if they are flying through the air to take a shot on the goal. This is known as a dive or jump shot. The poor goalkeeper usually doesn't stand a chance against these, and that's why teams score 25 to 40 goals a game.

JUMP SHOT
Powerful flying shot. Take that, keeper!

LIGHT SHOES
Players can wear any kind of sneakers, as long as they don't leave marks on the court.

A CLOSER LOOK

SMALL, SOFT BALL
Easy to grip and catch with only one hand

BASIC TRAINING

If you want to be an outfield player, jump high off the third step from the bottom on your staircase at home while throwing a honeydew melon with one hand toward the ground. Make sure you clean up afterward.

If you want to be a goalkeeper, get your family to throw balls at you as fast as possible from point-blank range. Wildly fling your arms and legs around, and if you are lucky, one of the balls might hit you. Save!

SKILLS NEEDED

Height is a big advantage in handball, especially if you're a goalkeeper. You also need to be fast and agile. Handball players spend a lot of time jumping in the air to hurl the ball at the goal, so an explosive shot helps too. To be a goalkeeper, you must be good at jumping jacks, spreading yourself as wide as possible, hoping that one day you might be able to save something.

A Bit of History

Handball was first played in Germany and Scandinavia in the late 1800s, but it took until 1917 for someone to write down the rules. Men's handball first appeared at the Summer Games in 1936, then didn't reappear until 1972. Women's handball made its Summer Games debut in 1976.

NO GLOVES
It's easier to throw the ball without gloves, but players sometimes wear strapping around their thumbs and fingers to prevent injury.

JUMPING JACK
Goalkeepers do this a lot to try to stop the other team from scoring.

Sound Like a Pro

"CENTER BACK"
A creative player who initiates play in both defense and attack. Usually the best player on the team.

"ASSAULT"
A body foul on another player

"SAVE"
Goalies sometimes make one of these! Make sure you cheer when it happens.

"PISTON MOVEMENT"
Attacking play that moves forward and backward

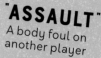

BEST EVER

There's a good spread of medals across Europe, but France is on top on the men's side with four medals, two of them gold.

On the women's side, Denmark has three golds, but both Norway and South Korea have six medals, with two golds each.

GOALIE PANTS
Goalkeepers wear these because it can get a bit chilly in those sports halls.

INJURIES
Ankle and knee injuries are common—there's even an injury called jumper's knee. You'll notice lots of players wearing kneepads and strappings.

CHANCE OF BECOMING A CHAMPION

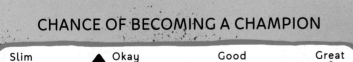

Handball is one of the most popular games in Europe, so the chances of becoming a pro there are slim. However, in some countries, it's not a very common sport.

UPSIDES
Handball is fast and fun, and there are plenty of chances to score lots of goals.

DOWNSIDES
Being a goalkeeper

FIELD HOCKEY

WHAT IS IT?

Two teams of 11 players try to hit a ball into their opponent's goal using a wooden stick.

The Rules

Using the flat side of their stick, players dribble, pass, flick, and sweep the ball along the ground toward the semicircle around their opponent's goal. Then they take a shot and hope to get it past the goalkeeper. The team with the most goals at the end of the game is the winner. Only the goalkeeper can touch the ball with their body, and players can't swing their stick around like they're going into battle.

INJURIES

Hand and forearm injuries are common because they're closest to the sticks. All the leaning down can also put pressure on your back.

A BIT OF HISTORY

There are carvings of ancient Greeks playing what looks like hockey from 510 BCE, but historians disagree about where the game came from. What we do know is the modern version of field hockey was developed in Great Britain in the 1800s and made it to the Summer Games in 1908 for men and 1980 for women.

Basic Training

Find a cane and a hard apple, like a Granny Smith. Then, using the stick, dribble the apple all the way home without kicking it or picking it up. Once you get there, whack it as hard as you can through the open front door. If you break something, blame the International Hockey Federation.

BANDANA

Very popular in field hockey. Players spend most of the time looking down, so the bandana keeps their hair out of their eyes.

A CLOSER LOOK

HARD PLASTIC BALL

Can travel at ferocious speeds of over 60 miles (100 kilometers) per hour. It has tiny bumps to keep it from skidding on a wet field.

BEST EVER

Men's field hockey is easily India's best sport, with 11 medals, eight of them gold. The women's teams from Australia and the Netherlands have won three golds each.

FIELD
Usually green or blue artificial turf with a covering of water or sand, to make the game quicker

GLOVE
Helps the player grip the stick and protects their hand from injury

Sound Like a Pro

"BULLY" or **"FACE-OFF"**
Two players tap each other's sticks and the ground three times. This is done to start or restart a game.

"RUSHER"
The player chosen to charge at the attacker taking a penalty corner

"HACKING"
Whacking another player's stick rather than the ball

"GREEN CARD"
A warning card, issued before the yellow and red cards

GOAL
Rectangular, with a backboard and sideboards

SHIN GUARDS
Getting hit on the shins with a wooden stick or hurtling ball really hurts. Shin guards help.

STICK
A J-shaped hook-bottomed stick, perfect for close ball control

GOALKEEPER
Dressed in so much protective clothing that it's hard to walk: helmet; chest, neck, and arm guards; padded shorts; huge leg guards; and big kicker boots

UPSIDES
Field hockey is fast, energetic, and a great team sport.

DOWNSIDES
Keeping up with the ball can be tiring, and the ball really hurts if it whacks into you.

SKILLS NEEDED
You need stamina to keep running up and down the field, as well as good hand-eye coordination. You must be able to make quick decisions, and bravery helps, too — especially if you're defending a penalty corner.

CHANCE OF BECOMING A CHAMPION

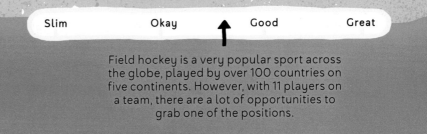

Slim   Okay   Good   Great

Field hockey is a very popular sport across the globe, played by over 100 countries on five continents. However, with 11 players on a team, there are a lot of opportunities to grab one of the positions.

Boccia

WHAT IS IT?

A sport for athletes with physical disabilities, in which players try to get their ball as close as possible to a target ball. It's a bit like lawn bowling, but better.

The Rules

Matches are divided into a number of ends, or frames. In each end, an athlete throws their set of balls as close as possible to the jack, or target ball. The player whose ball is closest to the jack after all the balls are thrown scores a point, and extra points for any other ball that they have nearer than their opponents' closest ball.

Balls can be thrown, chucked, rolled, or kicked in any way. You can even hurl it down like a football quarterback if you wish.

Individual players and pairs play four ends, and teams of three play six ends. After all ends have been played, the athlete or team with the highest score wins the match.

A CLOSER LOOK

BALLS
A set of six red or blue soft leather balls, which can roll but don't bounce, as well as a white target ball called a jack

NUMBERS
Athletes are identified by numbers attached to their wheelchairs or legs.

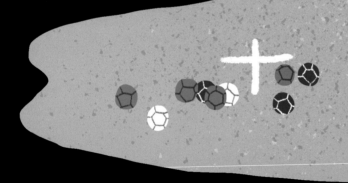

A BIT OF HISTORY

Boccia has its origins in ancient Greece and Egypt, where players threw large stones at a stone target. The Italians turned the game into something called bocce, which spread around the world; variations include bowls and pétanque. Boccia joined the Paralympics in 1984 and is one of two Paralympic sports that don't have a similar sport in the Olympics.

Sound Like a Pro

"SPOCKING" or "BOMBING"
Making a hard underarm throw aimed at directly hitting the jack or other balls

"KISS"
When a ball is touching the jack

"SKUNKED"
A player is skunked when they fail to score any points.

"PALLINO"
Another term for the jack

"CASINO"
Scoring all four points in one end

"JACK ADVANTAGE"
The edge given to the player who gets to throw the jack and the first ball

"LAGGING" or "POINTING"
Making an underarm throw that rolls a ball toward the jack

SKILLS NEEDED

Boccia is for players with conditions that affect motor skills. Players need to be strong to spend hours leaning over the side of the wheelchair, and their shoulders get sore. Mental toughness is also very important because players are under nail-biting pressure to land a ball just millimeters away from the jack. Boccia is also a great test of muscle control, strategy, and pinpoint accuracy.

UPSIDES

It's a top-notch strategy sport that is hard to master. It looks easy but it isn't. It's also a sport that men and women can play together.

DOWNSIDES

Boccia requires lots and lots of practice and stacks of concentration.

HEAD POINTER
Helps athletes who can't use their hands push the ball down the ramp

INJURIES

You'd be very unlucky if you got injured playing boccia. The referee measuring the ball distances is more likely to get injured by a stray throw.

WHEELCHAIR
Boccia doesn't require a special chair to play, so it's not an expensive sport to get involved with.

RAMP
Some athletes are allowed to use ramps to help roll the ball or an assistant if they can't move the ball on their own.

BEST EVER

Portugal tops the medal table with 26 medals, but South Korea has the most gold medals — 9 out of their 20.

BASIC TRAINING

Boccia is the perfect game to practice in your yard or a park, but you'll need to raid the fruit bowl first. Sitting in a chair, throw an orange across the grass. Then, aiming as best as you can, try to land six lemons as close as possible to the orange. And when you're done, make lemonade!

CHANCE OF BECOMING A CHAMPION

Slim   Okay   Good   Great

Tough but not impossible. Boccia is highly skilled at the top level, but it's a very popular sport and there are lots of opportunities to get involved. It's played in around 50 countries.

VOLLEYBALL

WHAT IS IT?

Two teams battle it out on either side of a high net, trying to keep a ball from hitting the floor.

BASIC TRAINING

Move your living room furniture out of the way, throw a beach ball in the air, and try to stop it from hitting the floor by whacking it with your hands clenched together. When your parents get home and see the state of things, hide behind the sofa.

A CLOSER LOOK

VERY HIGH NET
The net is 2.4 meters tall for men and 2.2 meters tall for women.

VOLLEYBALL
A softish bouncy ball

LIBERO
A specialized defensive player who wears a different color from everyone else on the team

KNEE PADS
To protect from grazes when players dive for the ball

FRONT ZONE
Where the attackers hang out

SLEEVELESS TOPS AND SHORTS
Usually lightweight cotton with a number on the back

The Rules

Indoor volleyball has two teams of six, who get up to three touches, or volleys, to keep the ball off the floor on their side of the net, and then land it on the floor on their opponent's side of the court. The first team to 25 points wins the set, and it's usually best of five sets. A team must also have two more points than the other team to win.

Beach volleyball has similar rules, but there are only two players on each team. It's played on a slightly smaller sandy court, with a softer, smaller ball, and it's best of three games.

Sitting volleyball is similar to indoor volleyball but has a smaller court and lower net, and players must have a part of their body, usually one butt cheek, touching the floor when playing a shot.

INJURIES
Shoulder and finger injuries are common, as is sunburn if you forget to put sunscreen on for beach volleyball.

BACK ZONE
Where the defenders hang out

A BIT OF HISTORY

Volleyball was invented in 1895 in the United States, as a less tough version of basketball. Its popularity quickly spread around the world. It debuted at the Summer Games in 1964. Beach volleyball was invented in 1915 and made its first appearance in 1996. The Paralympics added sitting volleyball in 1980 for men and 2004 for women.

Sitting Volleyball

PELVIS ON THE GROUND
At all times, otherwise you'll get a lifting foul.

REFEREE ON A PLATFORM
There are usually two referees; the senior one stands on a platform to get a good view.

ATTACK LINE
One-third of the way between net and end line

BEST EVER

In indoor volleyball, medals have been shared fairly evenly over the years, but the Soviet Union (USSR) is still at the top with 12 medals. The United States and Brazil have 10 medals each in both indoor volleyball and beach volleyball. Team USA's Misty May-Treanor and Kerri Walsh Jennings have won three gold medals. In sitting volleyball, Iran and Germany lead the way.

MAY-TREANOR AND JENNINGS'S MEDAL COUNT: 🥇 X3

Sound Like a Pro

"SPIKE"
To smash the ball into your opponent's court

"KONG"
A one-handed block

"SPATCH"
A hit to the ball that sends it somewhere unexpected

"SPALDING"
A really hard hit from a ball to a player's face or body

"CAMPFIRE"
When a serve lands between players because they didn't decide in time who should go for it

UPSIDES
Nothing beats leaping like a salmon above the net to smash down a powerful spike into your opponents' court. KABOOM — take that!

DOWNSIDES
Diving around to return the ball can give you floor burns or a mouthful of sand depending on which type of volleyball you play.

CHANCE OF BECOMING A CHAMPION

| Slim | Okay | Good | Great |

Many people enjoy messing around with a volleyball on a beach, but the game's not as popular when it comes to forming a team and taking it seriously. It is popular in eastern Europe and Brazil.

SKILLS NEEDED

Being tall is an advantage, but you also need to have lightning-quick reflexes to get in the right position to block, dig, set, and spike.

BASEBALL
and Softball

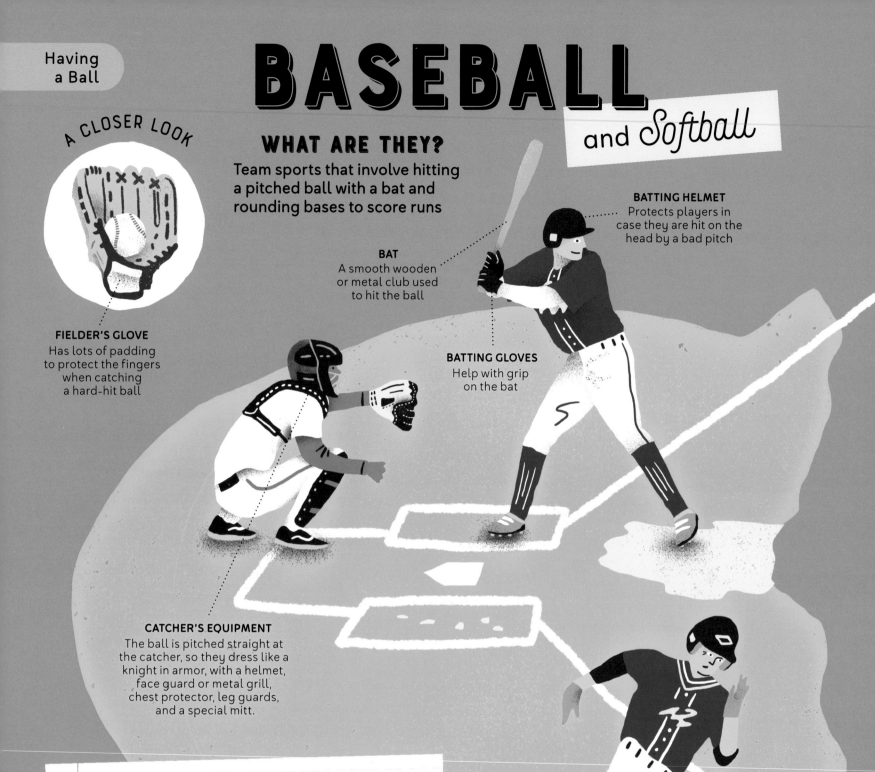

A CLOSER LOOK

FIELDER'S GLOVE
Has lots of padding to protect the fingers when catching a hard-hit ball

WHAT ARE THEY?
Team sports that involve hitting a pitched ball with a bat and rounding bases to score runs

BAT
A smooth wooden or metal club used to hit the ball

BATTING HELMET
Protects players in case they are hit on the head by a bad pitch

BATTING GLOVES
Help with grip on the bat

CATCHER'S EQUIPMENT
The ball is pitched straight at the catcher, so they dress like a knight in armor, with a helmet, face guard or metal grill, chest protector, leg guards, and a special mitt.

The Rules

Baseball is played by two teams of nine players; each team usually has nine turns at bat to score as many runs as possible. Players score runs by rounding three bases and returning to home plate. Once three players are out, that's the end of the team's turn at bat. Players are out if they swing and miss the pitched ball three times, if their ball is caught without hitting the ground, or if they're tagged while running between bases. One turn at bat for each team constitutes an inning.

The rules for softball are very similar, but the ball is bigger, the pitcher throws underarm, and a game has only seven innings.

SKILLS NEEDED

Baseball players need to be good at throwing, catching, and hitting. It helps if you are a fast runner, but if you hit the ball out of the park for an automatic home run, you can just jog around the bases blowing kisses to the crowd.

INJURIES

Throwing a ball at 90 miles (145 kilometers) per hour takes a lot of energy, and pitchers injure their shoulders and elbows a lot.

BALL

Cork ball with a stitched leather coat. A softball is slightly bigger than a baseball.

BASEBALL CAP

The cap's brim shields players' eyes from the sun.

BASIC TRAINING

Nice and simple. Get yourself a nice juicy grapefruit, throw it above your head, and as it comes down, thrash it with a stick as hard as possible over your neighbor's fence.

Sound Like a Pro

"DIAMOND"
The four bases are set up in a diamond formation.

"BEANBALL"
A pitch thrown at the batter's head, usually on purpose

"WINDUP"
The motion the pitcher makes before throwing the ball

"SLUGGER"
A player who hits a lot of home runs

"HEATER"
A really fast pitch

CLEATS

Players wear spiked shoes, or cleats, for stability and traction.

BEST EVER

Cuba has the most Olympic baseball medals, with five, three of them gold. The United States has won baseball gold only once but dominates in softball, winning every gold medal except one, in 2008, when Japan beat them in the final.

A Bit of History

Baseball, which has its roots in European sports like rounders and cricket, was developed in the United States in the 1840s. By the 1850s, it was already being referred to as America's national pastime. It debuted in the Summer Games in 1992 but hasn't always been included in recent years. Softball joined the Games in 1996 as a women's event but hasn't always been included, either.

UPSIDES

Hitting a home run out of the park is one of the biggest thrills in sports. And nobody can do anything about it! Baseball is also the only sport where you won't get yelled at for spitting.

DOWNSIDES

Baseball games can be long, and there's a lot of hanging around waiting for your turn at bat. When you're playing the outfield, the ball so rarely comes to you, you might fall asleep!

CHANCE OF BECOMING A CHAMPION

Slim	Okay	Good	Great

It depends where you come from. Baseball is extremely popular across the United States, Japan, and South Korea, so chances of getting picked there are low.

GOLF

WHAT IS IT?

Spending most of the day outside trying to hit a tiny white ball into 18 little holes with a variety of metal clubs

The Rules

A golfer has to whack their little ball into 18 different holes in the fewest hits (called strokes) as possible. To make the game harder, there are sandpits, lakes, rivers, woods, and hills for the ball to get lost in. Some courses in the US even have massive alligators that sometimes get in the way.

BASIC TRAINING

Get a small ball about the size of an apricot. Actually, why not just get an apricot? Then find a stick that has a sticky-out bit at the bottom. Hit the apricot as hard as you can across a field and into some deep undergrowth. Spend 30 minutes looking for the apricot, then give up and go inside.

SINGLE GLOVE
Often worn for better grip

CADDIE
Carries the player's golf bag around and offers advice and support. Tells them what they should have for lunch.

COLORFUL CLOTHING
Anything goes. If you want to wear a purple vest, lime-green pants, and yellow socks at the same time, then this is the sport for you.

INJURIES
Shoulder, elbow, and back pain is very common, although probably more so for the caddie, who has to carry your bag.

CLUBS
The different types of clubs are called woods, irons, wedges, and putters.

Sound Like a Pro

"WHIFF"
To attempt to hit the ball, but totally miss it

"PAR"
The standard number of strokes it should take to finish a hole. Usually three, four, or five.

"BOGEY"
One stroke over par. So not a good thing.

"DOGLEG"
A fairway with a sharp turn

"PLUS FOURS"
Baggy knickers that used to be all the rage in golfing wear

BEST EVER

There have only been five gold medals handed out (three for men and two for women), so nobody really dominates. USA and Great Britain have done well, and the current women's champion is South Korea's Inbee Park.

A CLOSER LOOK

FLAG
A very serious flag. Don't wave it around or other golfers will look down their noses at you.

GREEN
Special grass around a hole. It's like an expensive carpet, so don't go running and dancing on it.

HOLE
So small it has to have a big flag poking out of it so you can spot what you are aiming at from far away.

BALL
A small, hard ball covered in over 300 dimples, which help the ball travel farther. Usually white, but luminous colors are also popular, as they make balls easier to find.

BUNKER
Try to keep your ball out of these sandpits. Sadly, not a place for sand castles.

FAIRWAY
The part of the course between the tee and the green, surrounded by rough, which is easy to lose your ball (and your temper) in.

TEE
Drive your ball off the top of this little plastic or wooden stick at the start of every hole.

SKILLS NEEDED

Golfers come in all shapes and sizes. Because the caddie carries your bag and some golfers drive around in little buggies, you don't have to be super fit, like most other athletes.

To play golf, you need to be mentally tough because you're basically in a battle with yourself across 18 holes. If you're the kind of person who loses your temper when you burn your toast, then golf isn't for you.

A Bit of History

It is believed that golf started in Scotland in the 1400s, when players whacked a pebble around a course using a stick. However, some historians trace it back to an ancient Roman game called paganica. Golf debuted at the Summer Games in 1900. It made it to 1904 before disappearing off the event list for over 100 years and making a comeback in 2016.

UPSIDES

Golfers get to wear casual clothes, travel to play on some of the most beautiful courses in the world, and don't need to do any running.

DOWNSIDES

Golfers play in all weather. Trying to find your ball in the woods while it's cold and rainy is not fun. And there are more rules than in most sports.

CHANCE OF BECOMING A CHAMPION

Slim — Okay — Good — Great

World-class professional golfers enter the Olympics, so in order to qualify, you probably need to start winning tournaments now.

Shooting

SKEET
In skeet shooting, clay disks are fired from a machine called a trap; shooters need lightning-quick reactions to hit them.

WHAT IS IT?

Very serious athletes stand very still and fire rifles, shotguns, and pistols at teeny-tiny targets and hope they don't miss.

The Rules

Rifle and pistol shooting events are held on a shooting range, where competitors fire at targets 10, 25, and 50 meters away. Points are awarded depending on how close to the bull's-eye you get.

Skeet shooters fire shotguns at moving clay targets called pigeons that are pinged across the sky at different angles and directions. You've just got to keep hitting them—the more you miss, the trickier it is to get a medal.

A CLOSER LOOK

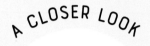

SPECIAL SHOOTING GLASSES
A complicated set of glasses with different lenses to help the eyes focus and blinders to block any distractions

CLOTHING THAT MAKES YOU LOOK LIKE YOU'RE FROM THE FUTURE
Everything is designed to stop even the slightest movement, like a puff of wind, from distracting you.

SHOTGUN
Shotguns have different length barrels depending on the event. Magnifying lenses are not allowed.

AIR RIFLE
Looks like a gun from outer space

INJURIES
Pain in the neck, back, hips, and knees is common because you have to stand and kneel for long periods of time and support a heavy rifle.

BASIC TRAINING

Find a room with a dirty mark on the wall, then stand on the other side of the room and stare at it for two hours without moving.

KNEE ROLLS
Shooters wear stiff canvas pants and jackets. The pants have nonslip rubber patches on the knees to keep the shooters steady when they're kneeling or lying down.

SKILLS NEEDED

Shooting is all about being cool, calm, and collected. If you're easily distracted by things like clouds, birds, wind, or someone coughing a mile away, then shooting probably isn't for you. You need to remain as still as a lamppost, be able to control your breathing, and not scratch your itchy chin. Good eyesight, great aim, stamina, strength, and nerves of steel are also crucial.

UPSIDES

Hitting a bull's-eye is a great feeling. Plus you get to dress like a cyborg.

DOWNSIDES

Shooting involves extreme pressure, and standing still and remaining calm can be very hard—especially if your opponents are trying to distract you by saying things like "Watch out for the baboon!"

DISTANCE

Rifle and pistol targets are usually 10, 25, or 50 meters away from the competitors, depending on the event.

RIFLE TARGET

Digital sensors in the target send information to the scorers. The bull's-eye is the size of your little fingernail.

PISTOL TARGET

You'll lose points if you accidentally hit someone else's target!

AIR PISTOL

The arm that holds the pistol must be straight and completely unsupported.

Sound Like a Pro

"FIRING LINE"
Where you stand to shoot

"TRAP"
The machine that fires the clay targets into the air

"PULL" or "HUP" or "READY"
Skeet shooters shout one of these terms to signal that the clay target may be released.

"MUZZLE"
The front end of the weapon, where the pellet, cartridge, bullet, or round leaves

BEST EVER

The USA dominates the shooting medal table, with 110 medals, 54 of them gold. American marksman and naval officer Carl Osburn won eleven shooting medals (five gold), from the Olympics in 1912, 1920, and 1924.

OSBURN'S MEDAL COUNT:

1 X5   2 X4   3 X2

A BIT OF HISTORY

The Chinese probably introduced guns to the world in the tenth century when they invented gunpowder. Then various weapons started appearing across the world, and soon armies swapped their bows and arrows for rifles and pistols.

Shooting became a sport around 500 years ago, when people realized it wasn't just for killing things and could be fun. It was one of the sports at the 1896 Summer Games.

CHANCE OF BECOMING A CHAMPION

Slim   Okay   Good   Great

Shooting obviously has a lot of restrictions. You can't just pick up a gun and start shooting at things—that might get you arrested. However, if you're taught properly, your chances increase greatly since it's not a sport that many people learn.

ARCHERY

WHAT IS IT?

Using a bow, competitors shoot arrows at a target a long way away. It's basically playing Robin Hood without the hiding in trees part.

Sound Like a Pro

"UPSHOT"
The last shot in an archery tournament

"LOOSE"
To release an arrow, letting it fly

"LITTLE JOHN"
Best friend of Robin Hood . . . Hang on, how did this get in here?

"QUIVER"
A case for holding arrows

"NOCK"
To fit an arrow into the bowstring

"FLETCHER"
Someone who makes arrows. So, anyone with the last name Fletcher has ancestors who were arrow makers.

A CLOSER LOOK

ARROW FLIGHTS
Once made of feathers, arrow flights are now made of plastic and help with speed and direction.

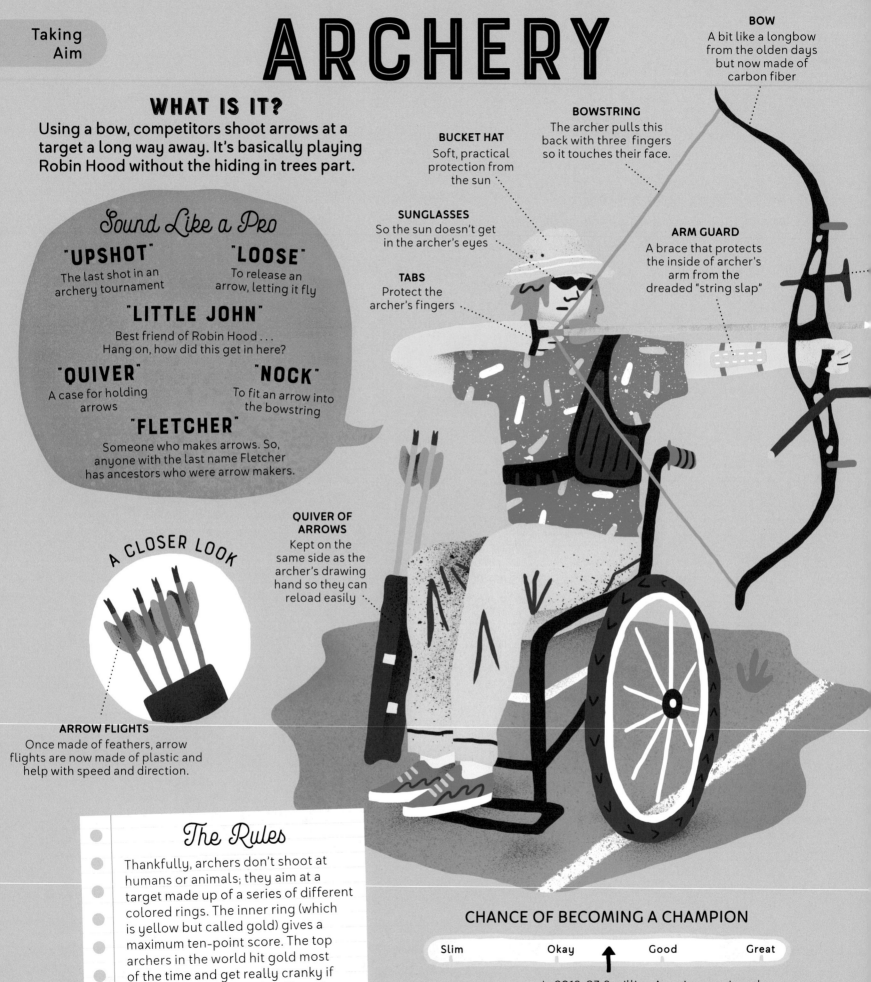

BUCKET HAT
Soft, practical protection from the sun

SUNGLASSES
So the sun doesn't get in the archer's eyes

TABS
Protect the archer's fingers

BOWSTRING
The archer pulls this back with three fingers so it touches their face.

BOW
A bit like a longbow from the olden days but now made of carbon fiber

ARM GUARD
A brace that protects the inside of archer's arm from the dreaded "string slap"

QUIVER OF ARROWS
Kept on the same side as the archer's drawing hand so they can reload easily

The Rules

Thankfully, archers don't shoot at humans or animals; they aim at a target made up of a series of different colored rings. The inner ring (which is yellow but called gold) gives a maximum ten-point score. The top archers in the world hit gold most of the time and get really cranky if they get a different color. They do not, however, shout "It's a bull's-eye!" when they hit it — that's for darts.

CHANCE OF BECOMING A CHAMPION

| Slim | Okay | ↑ | Good | Great |

In 2018, 23.8 million Americans enjoyed archery, so it's pretty popular.

A Bit of History

People have been using bows since the Stone Age, but mainly for hunting. Fed up with using it just to catch food, the ancient Egyptians turned it into a battlefield weapon and a sport. The first recorded sporting tournament was in China way back in 1027 BCE. So, archery is really, really, really old.

INJURIES

Archery is a relatively safe sport as it's noncontact and competitors are stationary. However, wrist, elbow, and shoulder injuries can happen due the constant force required when pulling back the bowstring. You could also get really hurt if you decided to wander around near the targets when people are practicing.

SKILLS NEEDED

A good aim, steady arms, mental toughness, and lots of patience. You need to be accurate but also consistent.

SIGHT
A rod with a viewfinder on the end that helps the archer aim at the target

DISTANCE
That's about the length of two and a half blue whales. (But it's measured with a tape measure, not an actual whale.)

70 METERS

TARGET
For maximum points, archers want to hit the gold center every time they shoot.

STABILIZER
Helps the archer hold the bow still

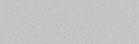

BASIC TRAINING

It's easy to set up targets in your backyard, but be sure to use a toy bow that fires plastic or wooden arrows with rubber stoppers. Don't use ones with metal tips — they're deadly weapons.

BEST EVER

The South Koreans are the true Robin Hoods of archery. It is their best Olympic sport. Since 1972, when archery returned to the Games after a 52-year break, they have won 39 medals, 23 of which were gold. It's not surprising, since children in Korean primary schools often have two-hour archery lessons as part of their day. Kim Soo-nyung has won the most medals for Korea.

KIM'S MEDAL COUNT:

🥇 X4   🥈 X1   🥉 X1

UPSIDES

Watching the arrow you've just shot fly through the air and hit a gold target a long way away is very satisfying. Plus, you can imagine what it must have been like being an archer back in the Middle Ages.

DOWNSIDES

Releasing an arrow is not as easy as you think. It's tough pulling the string back, and when you loose the arrow, it can give you a right old whack on the inside of your arm. And after all that, you may suddenly realize that your arrow has landed in a lake nowhere near the target.

BOXING

WHAT IS IT?

Two fighters stand in a ring, which is actually a square, and bash each other in the face and body until one of them is declared the winner.

The Rules

Boxing rules are constantly changing, and there are a lot of them because it's so dangerous, but essentially, male boxers fight three three-minute rounds, and women fight four two-minute rounds. The fighter who lands the most punches to their opponent wins the fight by a knockout, the referee stepping in to stop the fight, or the judges' decision.

Competitors may use only their fists to hit their opponent. Elbowing, headbutting, biting, and hair pulling all result in losing points or disqualification. Boxers also can't punch below the belt.

PROTECTIVE HEADGEAR

Since 2016, men don't have to wear headgear but women still do.

NO BEARDS

Beards and mustaches are banned.

PLAIN SHORTS

No fancy shiny shorts here — just plain red or blue.

SKILLS NEEDED

Boxers need to be tough, fit, and not bothered by getting whacked in the face. If you burst into tears when you fall, avoid this sport. Your size doesn't matter, though, because there are different weight divisions, including flyweight and featherweight. (You don't actually have to weigh as much as a fly or a feather. That would be silly.)

RING

Competitive boxing started in a chalk circle drawn on the floor. Now it's on a raised square platform, so it's easier to see the fight.

INJURIES

Concussions, brain injuries, broken bones, memory loss . . . the list goes on. Think of an injury, and a boxer could get it.

A BIT OF HISTORY

Hand-to-hand fighting has been around ever since Caveman Dave took a swing at his neighbor for stealing his woolly mammoth. It's so old the ancient Greeks made it part of their Games in 688 BCE. Men's boxing has been part of the modern Games since 1904, and women's boxing joined in 2012.

CANVAS

The padded floor of the ring — not used for painting

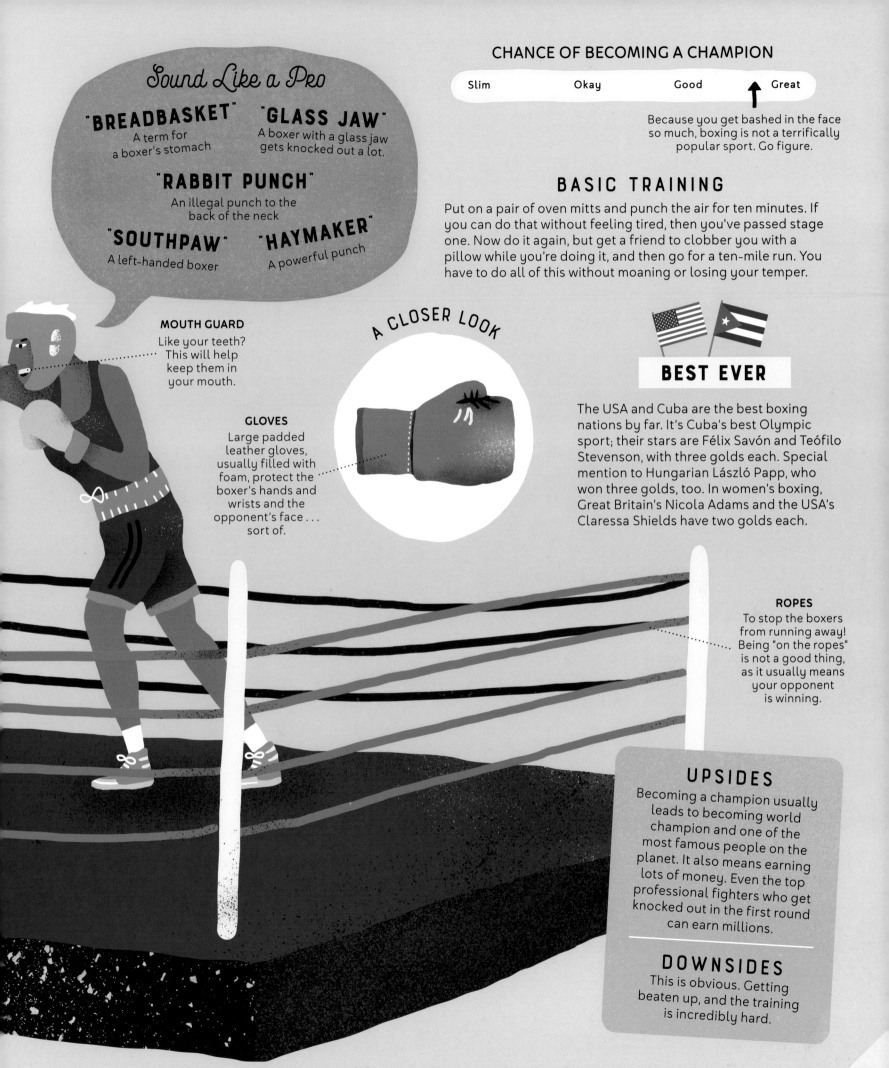

Sound Like a Pro

"BREADBASKET"
A term for a boxer's stomach

"GLASS JAW"
A boxer with a glass jaw gets knocked out a lot.

"RABBIT PUNCH"
An illegal punch to the back of the neck

"SOUTHPAW"
A left-handed boxer

"HAYMAKER"
A powerful punch

CHANCE OF BECOMING A CHAMPION

Slim	Okay	Good	↑ Great

Because you get bashed in the face so much, boxing is not a terrifically popular sport. Go figure.

BASIC TRAINING

Put on a pair of oven mitts and punch the air for ten minutes. If you can do that without feeling tired, then you've passed stage one. Now do it again, but get a friend to clobber you with a pillow while you're doing it, and then go for a ten-mile run. You have to do all of this without moaning or losing your temper.

MOUTH GUARD
Like your teeth? This will help keep them in your mouth.

GLOVES
Large padded leather gloves, usually filled with foam, protect the boxer's hands and wrists and the opponent's face . . . sort of.

A CLOSER LOOK

BEST EVER

The USA and Cuba are the best boxing nations by far. It's Cuba's best Olympic sport; their stars are Félix Savón and Teófilo Stevenson, with three golds each. Special mention to Hungarian László Papp, who won three golds, too. In women's boxing, Great Britain's Nicola Adams and the USA's Claressa Shields have two golds each.

ROPES
To stop the boxers from running away! Being "on the ropes" is not a good thing, as it usually means your opponent is winning.

UPSIDES

Becoming a champion usually leads to becoming world champion and one of the most famous people on the planet. It also means earning lots of money. Even the top professional fighters who get knocked out in the first round can earn millions.

DOWNSIDES

This is obvious. Getting beaten up, and the training is incredibly hard.

FENCING

WHAT IS IT?

Very polite sword fighting in a straight line.
It does not involve putting up a fence.

THE RULES

Fencers score points by hitting each other with their weapon. The one with the most points at the end of three rounds, or whoever gets to 15 points first, wins. However, it's not quite that simple. There are three different types of weapons (all very thin and long), with different rules for each one. Wheelchair fencers compete in wheelchairs that are fixed to the floor, so their bouts are very fast and tactical.

A BIT OF HISTORY

People have been fighting each other with swords for thousands of years, but fencing wasn't turned into a sport until the 1700s. A mask was invented, and the weapon's tip was flattened, because plunging a sword into someone's chest wasn't considered very sporting. Fencing first appeared at the Games in 1896, and wheelchair fencing was one of the sports at the first Paralympics in 1960.

BASIC TRAINING

Get a friend, go to the woods, and find two long, thin sticks. Lunge and prance toward each other with the very tip of your stick swords.

LAMÉ
The electric scoring jacket worn on top of the cotton jacket

JACKET
Usually made of tough cotton with a strap that goes between the legs to keep it in place. Probably not as padded as competitors might like.

LONG SOCKS THAT GO UP TO THE KNEE
This is not a scruffy sport, so fencers keep them pulled up.

HANDGUARD
A metal guard to protect the fencer's fingers

ÉPÉE
Fencers like to call it their weapon, but it's actually blunt and has no sharp edges.

SKILLS NEEDED

You should be handy with a weapon but also nimble on your feet because there's a lot of prancing back and forth. Shouting and yelling during the bouts is also a key skill, mainly to intimidate your opponent but also to try to convince a referee that you scored a point.

CHANCE OF BECOMING A CHAMPION

| Slim | Okay | Good | ▲ Great |

In most countries, fencing is not one of the most popular sports.

Sound Like a Pro

"EN GARDE" or "ON GUARD"
Spoken by the referee at the start of a bout to tell players to get into position

"APPEL"
A forward movement of the front leg, often done to disrupt the opponent

"DIRECTOR"
The referee

"SALLE"
The room where you do your fencing

"BLACK CARD"
The worst type of referee punishment in any sport. You've done something really bad if you get one of these, and it means expulsion from the tournament.

BEST EVER

Italy and France are the true masters at fencing, with 125 and 118 medals. Hungary is not bad, either, with 87 medals.

Edoardo Mangiarotti was the world's most successful fencer, and Italy's best-ever Olympian, with 13 medals. He started fencing at age eight and turned himself into a left-handed fencer because they are more difficult to fight against.

MANGIAROTTI'S MEDAL COUNT:  ①X6 ②X5 ③X2

UPSIDES
Successfully hitting someone with your weapon at the same time as they're trying to hit you is a great feeling, especially since it's very hard to do.

DOWNSIDES
The equipment is expensive, and everyone will constantly ask you if they can "have a quick try at your sword."

UNDERARM AND CHEST PROTECTORS

BREECHES
Also called knickers, these are short trousers held up by suspenders.

INJURIES
Even though weapons are blunt and you wear protective clothing, a heavy prod in the chest or a whack on the hand can still deliver some belting bruises. It is sword fighting, after all.

A CLOSER LOOK

FENCING MASK
This has a mesh front to protect the face and a bib that protects the neck.

EPIC FAIL
French fencer Enzo Lefort's cell phone fell out of his back pocket during a match against a German fencer. He went on to lose the bout.

Judo

WHAT IS IT?

Judo is a Japanese martial art in which competitors, known as judokas, try to throw their opponent to the floor. *Judo* means the "gentle way," but hurling your rival over your shoulder seems anything but gentle.

SKILLS NEEDED

Judokas can be all shapes and sizes, and competitors are placed in weight divisions. So if you're really small, you won't be battling against a massive judoka with arms made of steel. Brute strength is not that important, but you will need good balance, courage, and cunning.

The Rules

Judokas spend most of each four-minute judo bout seemingly trying to remove each other's jackets. But they are actually trying to throw their opponent on their back or trap them on the floor for 20 seconds so they can claim something called ippon, which gives you an automatic victory. There are lots of other throws that sound cool, but they're not as powerful as an ippon.

You can't kick or punch or poke your opponent in the face. Hair pulling, teeth grabbing, and wild screaming are also no-nos. You need to concentrate on throwing, grappling, and holding.

For Paralympians, only athletes with sight impairments can compete; they are divided into sight classes and weight divisions.

HYGIENE

All judokas must have short fingernails and toenails. Long hair must be tied up, and competitors must smell fresh. So make sure you take a shower before a match. Your opponent will win automatically if you turn up looking like you slept in the woods.

IPPON
(ee-pon)
Also known as "the perfect throw." If you manage to pull off one of these, then you automatically win the bout.

A BLUE JUDOGI
It's hard to see what is going on when two players wearing white are grappling, so one wears blue instead.

A CLOSER LOOK

BARE FEET
If you struggle tying your shoelaces, then judo is the perfect sport for you.

A BIT OF HISTORY

Judo looks like it should be thousands of years old—something the samurai warriors used to practice when they weren't spinning their swords around—but actually it was only created in 1882. Judo joined the Summer Games in 1964, and the 2020 Games include a mixed team event for the first time.

BASIC TRAINING

An important part of judo is knowing how to fall properly. There are several fall-breaking techniques, called ukemi (oo-kay-mee). A bed is the perfect place to practice falling—just make sure that no one is asleep in it first!

INJURIES

Back, shoulder, and knee injuries are most common. However, judo legend Yasuhiro Yamashita won gold in 1984 despite tearing a calf muscle in the quarterfinals!

Sound Like a Pro

"O-GOSHI"
(oh-goh-shee)
A powerful hip throw

"WAZA-ARI"
(wah-zah-ah-ree)
A near ippon;
earns half a point.

"KARI-ASHI"
(kah-ree-ah-shee)
A foot sweep

"MAITTA"
(mah-ee-tah)
The signal, made by tapping the mat twice, that a judoka is giving up the bout

"MATE"
(mah-tay)
The referee calls "Mate," meaning "Wait" if they spot a problem, usually to get judokas to fix their gi.

BEST EVER

Japan's Tadahiro Nomura won three gold medals in the lightweight division at three consecutive Games. His uncle won gold at the 1972 Summer Games, too. Ryoko Tani has five Olympic medals—two gold, two silver, and a bronze—and she's also won seven world titles. Unsurprisingly, as the inventor of judo, Japan dominates the medal table with 84.

NOMURA'S MEDAL COUNT:  X 3

THICK COTTON JACKET AND PANTS, CALLED A JUDOGI OR GI

The gi is secured around the waist by a colored belt, or obi, that shows how good you are.

REFEREE

A nicely dressed person who strolls around the judokas and makes hand gestures to award points or penalties

PROTECTIVE MATS CALLED TATAMI

These soft mats keep your bones from shattering into a thousand pieces.

UPSIDES

You don't have to be stacked with muscles to be a top judoka, plus there are some awesome takedowns in judo.

DOWNSIDES

If you don't care for being tossed in the air and landing with a thud, this may not be the sport for you.

CHANCE OF BECOMING A CHAMPION

Slim	Okay	Good	Great

Over 40 million people around the world practice judo, but chances are even slimmer if you are from Asia or France, since that's usually where the best judokas come from.

KARATE

WHAT IS IT?

The martial art that everyone thinks they know because they saw it in a movie once. Unlike how it might look in movies, real karate requires discipline, technique, control, and accuracy.

GI
(gee) (with a hard *g*)
A white pajama-like uniform, which is light and loose-fitting so you can move around easily

SKILLS NEEDED

Being able to shout "EEEEIIIIOOOOO . . . WHOOOOO . . . HIYA" while chopping at the air with your hand isn't quite enough. You need to be powerful, fast, strong, and very determined.

EYE CONTACT
As a sign of respect, keep your eyes on your opponent at all times.

KIAI
Let out your loud battle cry as you attack; it helps your motivation and strikes fear into your opponent.

GLOVES
They cover the top of your hands for protection.

BASIC TRAINING

Find a karate master and pester them relentlessly until they get so fed up with you, they agree to teach you karate for free. This is how it works in all they movies, anyway. Sadly the chances of finding a karate master just wandering around the supermarket are slim.

FOOT PROTECTORS
Soft, padded shoes to protect your feet

COLORED BELT
In the Olympics, karatekas wear either a red (aka) or blue (ao) belt, so you can tell them apart.

Sound Like a Pro

"OSU"
(oss)
A greeting of respect

"REI"
(ray)
A bow

"HAJIME"
(hah-jee-may)
Begin

"IPPON NUKITE"
(ee-pon noo-kee-tay)
A hand strike with one finger sticking out — oww

"NAKADA KEN"
(nah-kah-dah ken)
A punch with a knuckle sticking out — oww again

"MAKIWARA"
(mah-kee-wah-rah)
A padded punching board used in training

BEST EVER

Karate is making its first appearance in the Summer Games in 2020, so whoever wins gold will make history. **Japanese** karatekas are the hot favorites since they've won the most world championship gold medals, but France, Spain, and Italy are competitive, too.

INJURIES

The most common injuries are around the head and neck: cuts, bruises, a broken nose, headaches, concussions, and more. However, if your opponent shows the correct amount of control and technique, you will avoid any nasty injuries.

The Rules

There are lots of different styles of karate, but there are just two in the Summer Games: kata (kah-tah) and kumite (koo-mee-tay).

Kata is the version of karate with no opponent. Fighters, known as karatekas (kah-rah-tay-kahs), perform their attacking and defensive moves to the judges in a routine that lasts around two minutes. The judges pick the winner based on speed, strength, focus, breathing, balance, and rhythm. This is the karate that everyone thinks they can do in the mirror or showing off to their friends in the park.

Kumite is the fighting part of karate. Karatekas must strike, punch, and kick areas of their opponent's body to score between one and three points. The first to have eight points more than their opponent or more points at the end of the round is the winner.

UPSIDES

People are immediately impressed if you say you can do karate. If you can throw in a couple of ninja-style flying somersaults, you will become the coolest person at school.

DOWNSIDES

If you get it wrong, karate can really hurt. Plus, it requires lots and lots of practice and bowing.

REFEREE
The person in charge of the match

A BIT OF HISTORY

Karate's origins are very blurry, as it goes back thousands of years and could have come from India, China, or Japan. Traditional karate (which means "empty hand") started in Okinawa, an island that is now part of Japan, hundreds of years ago but didn't start spreading around the world until the 1920s. Martial arts movies in the 1960s and 1970s made it popular, and soon everyone thought they were an expert.

MAT
Matches take place on a mat that is 8 meters or about 26 feet long.

CHANCE OF BECOMING A CHAMPION

Slim   Okay   Good   Great

Over 100 million people are believed to practice karate around the world, but only about 10,000 do so at a high level. There are only 80 athlete slots at the Summer Games, so you will have to work hard to grab one of them.

BELTS

Different colored belts show experience, with colors varying depending on the karate style, but white is always the most basic and black is highest. To even get close to becoming an Olympian, you must have a black belt.

BLACK
As deadly as a venomous black mamba snake

BROWN
As ferocious as an angry brown bear

BLUE
As dangerous as an annoyed blue shark

GREEN
As scary as a fed-up green lizard

RED
As lethal as a hungry red squirrel

YELLOW
As terrifying as a tired yellow butterfly

WHITE
As frightening as a fluffy white rabbit

WRESTLING

WHAT IS IT?

A combat sport in which two athletes in singlets roll around on a mat cuddling each other until one of them can't move anymore

The Rules

There are two types of wrestling at the Summer Games: Greco-Roman and freestyle. Greco-Roman is only for men and allows you to attack only above the waist, with your upper body or arms. In freestyle, pretty much anything goes!

Your main aim is to pin your opponent's shoulders to the mat for one second, called a fall. You also get bonus points for holds and throws through the bout.

Matches are two periods of three minutes, but it ends if there's a fall or a difference of ten points (freestyle) or eight points (Greco-Roman). You can also win if your opponent gets three warnings for foul play or for being too defensive, also known as being boring.

A BIT OF HISTORY

Wrestling is one of the oldest sports and was included in the first Games when nobody wore any clothes. For the next couple of thousand years, various civilizations invented their own versions of wrestling, and now it's done by most children, and some adults, when they are arguing over who gets the TV remote control.

Wrestling joined the Summer Games in 1896, but women's wrestling only appeared in 2004.

BEST EVER

The USA has the most wrestling medals, with Russia, Japan, and Turkey ranking highly. Japan's Kaori Icho is the best Olympic freestyle wrestler ever, with four gold medals.

A WHITE HANDKERCHIEF
This is used for quickly wiping away any blood or snot, and you get a warning if you don't carry one at all times.

A CLOSER LOOK

SKILLS NEEDED

You need to be strong and powerful with a quick-thinking strategic mind to spot the opportunity to strike. Stay clear if you don't like getting really close to someone else's armpit.

REFEREE
The referee awards points, uses a whistle to start and stop the action, and is helped out by a judge and a mat chairman who sit off the mat.

MAT
A circular thick rubber mat that feels like a giant marshmallow

Wrestling is very popular in Turkey, Mongolia, and the countries that surround Russia. However, because of the popularity of professional wrestling, like WWE, it is now considered to be a dying art. So, this is your chance. What are you waiting for?

Sound Like a Pro

"SQUEEEEEZE"
The crowd shouts this to encourage the wrestler on top to hold on to the wrestler who is trying to escape.

"FIVE"
Throwing an opponent feet over head, which gets you five points

"TAKEDOWN"
When you take your opponent down to the mat and gain control

"CAULIFLOWER EAR"
When your ear gets all lumpy due to constant bashing

BASIC TRAINING
A younger brother or sister can be your perfect training partner. Create a totally unnecessary argument, like who gets the last of the good cereal, and then wrestle for it until you've managed to get both their shoulders on the carpet. Remove the cereal from their hand and then eat it. Then get your mom to flap a tea towel at you to cool you down—wrestling is a sweaty business.

SLIPPERY GRIP
Covering yourself in grease so you can slip out of your opponent's grip is banned.

SHOOTING SLEEVE
Thinner than a knee pad, this helps wrestlers slide over the mat.

SHORT NAILS
So you can't slice your opponent

MOUTH GUARD
Like your smile? Wear one of these.

SINGLET
One contestant wears red; the other wears blue.

KNEE PADS
Protect against knee injuries, especially as you spend a lot of time crouched or on the floor.

WRESTLING SHOES
These are the only required piece of equipment, but to keep everyone from laughing, you might want to buy a singlet, too.

UPSIDES
Battling your opponent, tactically outthinking them, and then throwing or pinning them to the floor is the ultimate form of battle chess.

DOWNSIDES
If you don't like getting your face smooshed into the floor or covered in someone else's sweat, stay on the sofa.

INJURIES
You name it and you'll get it in wrestling. Bruises, sprains, cuts, fractures, and concussions—wrestling has them all.

TAEKWONDO

WHAT IS IT?

A combat sport in which two fighters try to kick or punch each other in the body or head to score points

The Rules

There are three two-minute rounds, with a minute's break in between, when coaches get to flap a towel in their athlete's face to cool them down. Judges award points for the more challenging and technical kicks and punches: a normal body blow gets one point, a kick to the head gets two, and knocking down an opponent gets three. Plus you get an extra point for doing any of these moves while spinning.

Points are taken away for fouls like attacking the face, punching the head, pulling an opponent to the ground, stepping over the mat boundary, and turning one's back on an opponent.

The athlete with either a knockdown or the most points at the end of three rounds wins.

BASIC TRAINING

Do lots of stretches to warm up, then put a balloon on the roof of your dad's car and see if you can leap up, spin, and kick it off. If you smash the windows or put a big dent in the door, run and hide under your bed for three months until he has calmed down.

PROTECTIVE CLOTHING

Athletes wear headgear, a mouth guard, arm and shin pads, and body and groin protectors.

DOBOK

(doh-bohk)
A white V-necked top and loose pants

HOGU

(hoh-goo)
Padded chest protector in red or blue that fits over the shoulders and is laced together at the back. This is the most common scoring zone.

A CLOSER LOOK

ELECTRONIC SOCKS

Sensors in the socks help record kicks' accuracy and power. Don't put them in the washing machine.

HEADGEAR

As kicks to the head are one of the main moves, protective headgear is one of the main pieces of equipment.

INJURIES

Even with all the padding, taekwondo can still sometimes hurt. The most common injuries are muscle strains, but kicks to the head can lead to neck injuries or concussions.

EPIC FAILS

Cuban athlete Ángel Matos was so angry at being disqualified from the bronze medal match at the 2008 Summer Games that he kicked the Swedish referee in the face. Matos, who had won gold at the 2000 Games, was banned from the sport for life.

Sound Like a Pro

"KYUNGNET"
(KYONG-nyeh)
Bow. Make sure you do this before every fight.

"KIHAP"
(kee-AHP)
Shout this when kicking or punching

"SHIJAK!"
(TSHEE-jahg)
Referees shout this to start a bout.

"CHAGI"
(CHAH-gee)
Kick

A BIT OF HISTORY

Taekwondo was developed after World War II by Korean martial arts masters. *Tae* means "foot," *kwon* means "fist," and *do* means "way of," so *taekwondo* means "the way of the foot and the fist" or "the way of kicking and punching."

It's now practiced in almost 200 countries across the globe and became a sport at the Summer Games in 2000.

CHANCE OF BECOMING A CHAMPION

| Slim | Okay | Good | Great |

Each country is allowed to enter only one athlete per weight category, so basically, you need to be the best fighter in your whole country. But it is a growing sport, so if you get involved now, you could have a chance.

SKILLS NEEDED

You need to be brave, strong, stretchy, and agile to become a good taekwondo fighter. If you can't touch your toes or lift your leg easily onto the kitchen table, then a flying spinning kick will be impossible. You don't need to be bursting with muscles, since athletes are put into weight categories: fly, feather, middle, and heavyweight.

COLORED BELT
You have to have a first-degree black belt or above to compete in the Olympics. The more markings you have on your black belt, the higher your rank.

BEST EVER

South Korea, where the sport was invented, has the most medals with 19, 12 of those gold. China is next with 10.

The USA's Steven Lopez and Iran's Hadi Saei have three medals each, both with two golds. Saei is Iran's most successful Olympian and started taekwondo when he was just six years old. South Korea's Hwan Kyung Seon is the first woman to win three taekwondo medals (two gold and one bronze).

MAT
Matches are fought on an octagonal mat that is 8 meters in diameter.

HWAN'S MEDAL COUNT: X2 X1

UPSIDES

Taekwondo is fast, furious, and great to watch. It rewards attacking shots, so athletes are always looking to pull off the spinning head kick.

DOWNSIDES

It takes a lot of work to learn all the moves and get them right.

45

Aquatics
SWIMMING

WHAT IS IT?

Being the fastest person to swim up and down a really long pool by moving your arms and legs in different ways

The Rules

Swim faster than everyone else until you reach the finish.

SHORTS CALLED JAMMERS FOR MEN
The torso and lower legs must remain bare.

A ONE-PIECE SWIMSUIT FOR WOMEN
These are made from a high-tech material that reduces drag in the water.

EAR PLUGS
Some swimmers wear plugs in their ears to keep water from getting in.

START BLOCK
Some races start with swimmers diving in from a little platform above their lane.

LANE ROPES
The pool is divided into lanes by ropes, held up by plastic floaters, stretched between each end.

NO ASSISTANCE
Paralympic swimmers are not allowed prostheses or assistive devices to help them in the pool, so these need to be removed before they jump in.

THE EVENTS

BREASTSTROKE

This is the slowest stroke. To do breaststroke, you need to perfect your frog-leg kicks and imagine your hands are scooping out a bowl of oatmeal and then throwing it behind you.

FREESTYLE

You can do any stroke you like in freestyle, but so far nobody has won a medal doing the doggy paddle. Front crawl is the fastest stroke—swimmers hardly take a breath.

BACKSTROKE

Backstroke is swimming on your back, with your arms going around and around like a windmill.

BUTTERFLY

This is the most exhausting and difficult stroke, with a lot of splashing from both your arms and legs.

UPSIDES

It's low impact on the body and great for keeping fit. Pools are nice and warm, and it's great if you need a bath.

DOWNSIDES

Early-morning starts. Most wannabe top swimmers are still in school, so they have to start training before school starts. Also, your career is short, as swimmers usually retire in their twenties.

A Bit of History

Swimming was invented after people discovered that too many of them were drowning when they tried to walk underwater.

Despite having been around for thousands of years, swimming didn't become a racing sport until the nineteenth century. It was at the first modern Games, in 1896, and first Paralympics, in 1960. Just to be different, backstroke didn't join until 1900 and women's swimming joined in 1912.

NO HAIR ON YOUR BODY

You are basically trying to make yourself as smooth and slippery as possible, like a dolphin.

A CLOSER LOOK

BASIC TRAINING

Fill a sink with water and dunk your head into it. After about ten seconds, turn your head to the side so your mouth is out of the water and take a gulp of air. Do this until your mom tells you to stop splashing water all over the floor.

GOGGLES AND CAP

Caps aren't compulsory, but most swimmers wear them. Plastic goggles help swimmers see underwater and protect their eyes from stinging chemicals.

Sound Like a Pro

"TUMBLE TURN"
An underwater somersault done at the end of a length to turn around quickly

"PB"
Personal best for a stroke and distance

"OPEN TURN"
A two-handed touch turn used in breaststroke and butterfly

"DOLPHIN KICK"
Whipping the legs while keeping your feet together, used in butterfly.

BEST EVER

Team USA has over 550 medals, 246 of which are gold, and over 680 medals at the Paralympics. That's a lot of medals!

Michael Phelps is the king of the swimmers and the most successful Olympic athlete ever. He has won 28 medals, 23 of them gold. His nicknames are the Flying Fish and the Baltimore Bullet (because he comes from Baltimore, Maryland, and swims as fast as . . . well, you can guess the rest).

American Paralympic swimmer Trischa Zorn has 55 medals, 41 gold, and is the most successful Paralympian of all time.

ZORN'S MEDAL COUNT: ① X41 ② X9 ③ X5

INJURIES

Since it's very hard to break a bone in the water, swimmers mostly just get muscle injuries. However, if you choose the backstroke, you will probably hit your head against the wall a few times. So expect a bruised head.

CHANCE OF BECOMING A CHAMPION

| Slim | Okay | Good | Great |

Low because swimming is very popular across the world and can be an essential life skill.

AQUATICS
Diving

WHAT IS IT?

Leaping off a high board, performing a series of elaborate acrobatics, then landing perfectly in a pool without making a big splash

THE RULES

Diving is very simple. You dive a number of times to score as many points as possible. The diver with the most points wins. The scoring is where it gets tricky, as it's based on factors including difficulty of the dive, takeoff, and splash, and points are deducted from a perfect score of ten. So just showing up and doing a cannonball won't win you any medals.

SHAMMY
No diver should be without a tiny towel for staying dry between dives.

A Bit of History

People have been jumping off cliffs to prove how tough they are since ancient times, but the activity didn't turn into a competition until the 1880s. Various forms of diving (plain, fancy, and high-board) started appearing in the Summer Games in the early 1900s, but the types of diving we see today (springboard and platform) didn't join the roster until 1928. Synchronized diving (which involves two people diving at the same time) joined in 2000.

A CLOSER LOOK

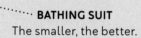

BATHING SUIT
The smaller, the better.

BASIC TRAINING

You'll need to learn and practice at a pool that has a diving board. If you're feeling brave, climb to the top and peer over the edge. If your legs don't turn to jelly, jump off feetfirst. If that wasn't too bad, do it again and again. . . .

3-METER SPRINGBOARD
A super springy board used for bouncing as high as you can to pull off awesome acrobatics in the air

UPSIDES

Diving is one of the most popular spectator sports at the Olympics, and if you get it right, it looks very impressive.

DOWNSIDES

The fear factor is huge. Getting your dive wrong and smacking into the water can also make you look a bit silly, and it hurts.

"SMACK"
To hit the water at the wrong angle. Ouch!

"RIP"
To enter the water vertically with hardly any splash

"BAIL"
To pull out of a move in midair, usually ending with a smack

INJURIES
Although the sport may look dangerous, nasty diving injuries are quite rare. Divers can get bruising from bad smacks, as well as shoulder, back, and arm injuries.

10-METER PLATFORM
As high as two giraffes standing on top of each other (something giraffes do only when humans aren't looking)

BEST EVER

The USA has the most Olympic diving medals, with a whopping 139, but in recent years China has started to dominate, especially in women's diving. One of the youngest-ever diving champions, Fu Mingxia, has won five Olympic medals. She collected her first at age 13, and that was off the 10-meter platform. Wow.

FU'S MEDAL COUNT: (1) X4 (2) X1

PIKE POSITION
When the diver bends their body at the waist, with straight legs and pointed toes. Nothing like the fish.

EPIC WIN

US diver Greg Louganis cracked his head on the board in the middle of one of his dives at the 1988 Games. He got a concussion but still went on to win gold!

CHANCE OF BECOMING A CHAMPION

Slim	Okay	Good	Great

Diving is not a common sport at schools even though some elite divers are as young as 14. People usually start with gymnastics or trampolining before moving on to diving if they're brave enough.

REALLY DEEP POOL
To make diving safe, diving pools, also called diving wells or tanks, are deeper than regular swimming pools. For even more safety: no sharks!

SKILLS NEEDED

The most important skill needed for diving is bravery. If you conquer the high board and leap off the top, you'll be traveling toward the water at around 35 miles (55 kilometers) per hour. That's seriously scary.

You also need to be good at gymnastics, acrobatics, or dance. Some dives even start with a handstand, so get practicing!

AQUATICS
WATER POLO

WHAT IS IT?

A team sport in which you throw a ball around a swimming pool to try to score as many goals as possible

SWIMMING POOL
The pool is all deep end, so you can't touch bottom. It's usually 20–30 meters long and 10–20 meters wide, with floating goals 3 meters wide and 0.9 meters tall.

Sound Like a Pro

"SKIP SHOT"
A powerful shot aimed into the water so it skips across the pool and (the player hopes) into the goal

"DRY PASS"
A pass thrown and caught without the ball touching the water

"TANK"
Another name for the pool

"DONUT"
A goal scored over the goalie's head and through their outstretched arms

"CHERRY PICKING" or **"SEAGULLING"**
When the defending team leaves one player in an attacking position, waiting to strike on goal

A MOUTH GUARD
Water polo can be violent, and you need your teeth to eat afterward.

BASIC TRAINING

Go to your nearest swimming pool and tread water for 30 minutes without touching the sides. Then get a friend to tackle you underwater as you try to throw a ball one-handed down the other end of the pool. Easy!

TIGHT, LIGHT SWIMSUITS
Suit-grabbing fouls are common, so swimsuits need to be tough.

THE RULES

Two teams of seven (including a goalie) have to score the most goals by throwing a ball into their opponent's net using only one hand. Only the goalie can use two hands. There are lots of fouls in water polo—one is even called a brutality—and players who commit fouls spend time in a sin bin.

A match is four quarters of eight minutes, but they can go on for much longer, as the clock is stopped when the ball is not in play. Teams only get 30 seconds for each attack.

A Bit of History

Water polo began in Britain in the mid-1800s as rugby in water. It was basically two teams beating each other up in a river or a lake as they tried to get a rubber ball to the other side. Players would hide the ball in their swimsuits, dunk other players heads underwater, and wrestle. It was mayhem until the introduction of stricter rules at the 1900 Games. Women's water polo was added 100 years later.

SKILLS NEEDED

You need to be a strong swimmer who is very good at treading water and doesn't mind getting splashed and bashed up.

A CLOSER LOOK

SWIM CAP
This has your number on it to show your position.

GOALIE'S CAP
A different color from the rest of their team's caps

EAR PROTECTORS
To prevent your ears from getting torn off and to keep water out

UPSIDES

You don't have to swim in a boring straight line, like in swim racing. Plus, water polo is fast and furious.

DOWNSIDES

Most top players are really muscular, so getting knocked around will hurt.

INJURIES

A ball in the face, battered ears, nail scratches, swallowing lots of pool water, and itchy eyes because water polo players don't wear goggles!

BEST EVER

Hungary reigns supreme, with 15 medals, nine of which are gold. The United States tops the medal table in the women's event, with two golds out of five medals.

CHANCE OF BECOMING A CHAMPION

Slim   Okay   Good   Great

If you live in Africa or Asia, your chances are very high. Countries in these continents have never won a medal and sometimes don't even bother entering. Chances are slimmer if you live in Eastern Europe because water polo is a big deal there.

AQUATICS

Artistic Swimming

WHAT IS IT?

Gymnastics and ballet in a swimming pool, in sparkly costumes, all to music. It used to be called synchronized swimming, but they changed the name because no one could spell it.

A SPARKLY COSTUME
Swimmers wear beautifully decorated swimsuits to match their beautiful choreography.

HAIR GEL
Swimmers use gel to plaster their hair to their head so it doesn't move during their performance.

NO GOGGLES
So you can make eye contact with the judges at all times

INJURIES
Swimmers can get back and hip injuries from all the dance moves, plus they probably swallow a lot of water.

LOTS OF DIFFERENT FACIAL EXPRESSIONS
"Grinning like a monkey that has just stolen the last bag of chips" seems to be the most popular.

The History Bit

Kids have been showing off underwater handstands to their moms forever. In the early twentieth century, some swimmers decided to get all fancy with their moves and call it water ballet. They performed elaborate routines in shows, at the World's Fair, and in movies. A sport then began to be developed, which joined the Summer Games as synchronized swimming in 1984.

NOSE CLIP
Swimmers can stay underwater for a really long time thanks to a special clip that prevents water from going up their nose.

NO TOUCHING THE BOTTOM
This makes all the lifts even more impressive.

The Rules

Artistic swimming and rhythmic gymnastics are the only Olympic sports open exclusively to women. Artistic swimmers perform entertaining routines to music, with judged moves both below and above the water.

There are two events: a duet event, with two swimmers, and a team event, with eight. Each event involves two routines: a technical routine, which lasts just under three minutes, and a free routine, which lasts three to four minutes.

Judges score routines on a scale of one hundred. They look at how well swimmers do their moves, how synchronized the moves are, how hard the tricks are, and at the routine's overall artistic impression.

BEST EVER

Russia has ten team Olympic gold medals, with Anastasia Davydova, Natalia Ishchenko, and Svetlana Romashina having won five each. Japan has the most medals, with 14, but none of them are gold.

BASIC TRAINING

Put on a swimsuit, get in the bath with a sibling or friend, and copy each other's movements for three minutes. Then perform your routine for some grown-ups while smiling the biggest smile you can smile. If they don't like it, splash them.

UPSIDES

Artistic swimming looks spectacular. Considering most people can't remember what they ate for breakfast, these swimmers have to remember and time their complicated routines perfectly, while spending most of the time underwater holding their breath. Amazing skills.

DOWNSIDES

There's a lot of training, and the added pressure of knowing that one mistake could ruin the routine for everyone else. You also have to spend hours in the pool getting very close to your teammates' feet and probably getting wrinkly skin.

A CLOSER LOOK

UNDERWATER MUSIC
A speaker under the water helps the swimmers keep in time with the music.

LOTS OF WATERPROOF MAKEUP AND DECORATIVE HAIR CLIPS
Artistic swimmers wear heavy theatrical make-up so the judges can see their expressions from far away.

SKILLS NEEDED

You need to be flexible and strong, with great musical timing and good gymnastic ability. It helps to have lungs the size of a whale. Oh, and being a good swimmer is pretty essential.

Sound Like a Pro

"BOOST"
A fast headfirst leap out of the water

"SCULLING"
Hand movements that help balance and propel the body

"EGGBEATER"
Treading water by rotating your legs in different directions

"DECKWORK"
The dance moves performed before getting into the water

CHANCE OF BECOMING A CHAMPION

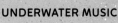

| Slim | Okay | Good | Great |

If you're a mermaid, you've got a great chance of winning a medal.

CANOE

WHAT IS IT?

Paddling a thin pointy boat as fast as you can to beat the other people in the race. Canoeing at the Summer Games includes sprint and slalom racing in both canoe and kayak.

A BIT OF HISTORY

Indigenous people around the world have been making canoes for millennia. The oldest known canoe dates to about 8,000 BCE. Kayaks were originated by Inuit, Aleut, and Yupik hunters and are traditionally made from sealskin stretched over a wood or whalebone frame.

SKILLS NEEDED

It's all about upper-body strength. Sprinters need loads of stamina, too, especially over the longer distances. You also need great skill and balance to keep your canoe or kayak from flipping over and throwing you out.

INJURIES

Shoulder and wrist injuries are most common, as is swallowing a lot of water.

The Rules

Canoe and kayak sprint couldn't be simpler. It's a straight race to the finish line on a flat stretch of water.

Slalom is much trickier. Competitors weave their way between poles, called gates, down whitewater rapids to get to the finish line. To make it even harder, some of the gates are upstream, so racers have to paddle back up the rapids to go through them. Penalty time is added if racers touch the gates, fail to go through them, or go through them the wrong way. The paddler with the fastest time at the end wins.

A CLOSER LOOK

BUOYANCY AID
Slalom Olympians wear life vests to keep them afloat if they get thrown into the rapids.

CANOE PADDLE
Single-bladed, with a T-shaped handle

CANOE
An open-topped boat for one or more paddlers, who fully kneel in slalom and kneel on one knee in sprint

BEST EVER

Hungary is at the top of the medal table with 80 medals, followed by Germany with 70. The best paddler is Germany's Birgit Fischer, who has won 12 medals, over six Summer Games. She won her first medal when she was 18 and her last at age 42!

FISCHER'S MEDAL COUNT:

BASIC TRAINING

Fill up your bath and get in wearing all of your clothes. Pick the biggest spoon you can find from the kitchen, plunge it into the water, and do a stroke on the left, then a stroke on the right. Repeat until you get really tired.

KAYAK PADDLE
Double-bladed and longer than a canoe paddle

HELMET
Protects the racer's head as they twist and turn through all the gates

KAYAK
A closed-top boat for one or more paddlers, who sit inside the kayak with their legs stretched out in front of them

COCKPIT COVER OR SPRAY DECK
Keeps water from coming into the kayak

GATES
Paddlers must go upstream through some hanging gates and downstream through others.

UPSIDES

Zipping through the water at high speed or testing yourself against powerful rapids is exhilarating. If you're in a boat with two or four paddlers, it can be a great team sport, too.

DOWNSIDES

If you don't like getting wet, then you'll be much happier watching from the riverbank.

Sound Like a Pro

"CAPSIZE"
To overturn a boat

"EDDY"
Water flowing differently from the main current

"SWAMP"
To fill with water (not recommended for canoes and kayaks)

CHANCE OF BECOMING A CHAMPION

Slim	Okay	Good	Great

Not many people own a boat or live near rapids.

SURFING

A CLOSER LOOK

LEASH
Ties around your ankle, calf, or wrist and keeps the board from escaping if you fall

WHAT IS IT?
Riding a pointy board on a huge wave while trying to look incredibly cool

SUNSCREEN
Important to protect surfers from the harsh sun

HAIR CARE
Don't spend hours on your hair before you go surfing, because it's going to get wet.

BOARD WAX
This looks like white chocolate (but don't eat it — it tastes nasty). It's rubbed all over the board to give you more grip.

CRUNCHER
A massive wave that is really hard to ride

The Rules

Surfers compete in groups of four and, depending on conditions, get around 20 to 30 minutes to ride any of the waves that roll up.

Only one surfer is allowed to ride any given wave, so competitors must follow right-of-way rules in the water.

Judges score each competitor, taking into consideration the types and difficulties of maneuvers, as well as speed, power, and flow. A surfer's two highest scores count, and the two top scorers in each heat advance to the next round.

A BIT OF HISTORY

Surfing has its origins among Polynesian people in the Pacific islands. Polynesians who migrated to the Hawaiian islands brought surfing with them, and there it developed and became an integral part of the culture: a fun pastime for children and, for adults, a display of daring, skill, and mastery. Hawaiian Duke Kahanamoku, an Olympic swimming medalist in the early 1900s, helped popularize the sport by giving exhibitions around the world.

INJURIES

Falling into water doesn't usually hurt, does it? It does when it involves a massive wave crashing down on you. Surfing is dangerous, and big cuts, head injuries, concussions, shoulder injuries, and bruising are common. Shark bites are very rare, unless you're a character in a movie.

BASIC TRAINING

Don't get in the water. Lay an ironing board on the floor and lie on top of it. Then practice jumping up on it — this is called a pop-up. It's a bit like a mini push-up. Do this for about an hour. Once you're standing on the board, get someone to try to tip you off it by vigorously rocking the board back and forth.

Sound Like a Pro

"AMPED"
Excited

"GOOFY-FOOT"
A surfer who rides with their right foot forward

"WEDGE"
A really steep wave

"GROMMET"
A beginner

"STICK"
Another name for a surfboard

"SHAKA"
A hand gesture with your little finger and thumb sticking out. It can mean lots of things, including "hello," "cool," "okay," or "hang loose."

"WIPEOUT"
A fall off the board, usually headfirst in a spectacular fashion

SURF STABILIZERS
Fins underneath the board to keep it steady on the waves

WETSUIT
Surfers wear special suits to keep them warm in the water.

LIGHTWEIGHT SURFBOARD
Made of fiberglass, with a pointy end to make it easier to maneuver

SOUP
Foam or white water from a broken wave

BEST EVER

World champion surfers have tended to hail from Australia, the United States (including Hawaii, which competes separately from the US in World Surfing League tournaments), and Brazil.

SKILLS NEEDED

You'll need balance, strength, and the ability to handle lots of salty water smashing into your face and up your nose.

UPSIDES

Riding a huge wave is a massive thrill, and you'll look like the coolest person on the planet.

DOWNSIDES

Downsides include falling in, swallowing lots of water, calm weather with no waves, and the occasional shark.

CHANCE OF BECOMING A CHAMPION

Slim	Okay	Good	Great

There are not many slots available in surfing competitions, so you need to be really good.

Rowing

WHAT IS IT?

Facing backward and using big sticks, or oars, athletes power a long thin boat across flat water toward a finish line as fast as they possibly can.

A THIN RACING BOAT
The length of the boat depends on how many rowers it will be carrying—from one to nine.

SLIDING SEATS
The seats go backward and forward when you row.

SIMPLE CLOTHING
Some shorts, a tank top, and maybe a cap or some sunglasses

BOW
Usually the smallest in the boat, the bow is responsible for stability, direction, and shouting things like "The other boats are coming!"

OARLOCK
Helps to keep the oars in place

A MASSIVE OAR
Oars can be more than twice as tall as the rowers. Rowers use one oar for sweeping and two for sculling.

INJURIES
Shoulder, back, and forearm injuries are the most common, but you will get blisters on your hands and feet too.

Skills Needed

Rowers are usually tall, strong, and incredibly fit and powerful, with tanks of stamina. There's still a place for you on a rowing team if you're small, though—as a cox. However, you need to be loud and good at leading a boat full of huge rowers.

BASIC TRAINING

Sit on your kitchen floor with a broomstick in your hands at a right angle. Then lean forward and backward moving the stick up and down the floor until you're sweaty and out of breath. Make sure you get someone to splash you with water and shout orders as you are kitchen-rowing. When you've finished, ask your mom for some extra pocket money for sweeping the floor.

A BIT OF HISTORY

Rowing is a very old form of transport, popular with the ancient Egyptians, Romans, and Greeks. The British turned it into a racing sport in the 1600s, and it grew from there, especially in English schools and universities, with the first Oxford-Cambridge boat race in 1829.

Rowing featured in the 1896 Summer Games, but the event was called off due to bad weather and a stormy sea. They don't usually row in the sea nowadays because it is too unpredictable.

Women's rowing didn't join the Games until 1976, and it didn't feature at the Paralympics until 2008.

A CLOSER LOOK

SHOES
Rowing shoes come clipped into the boat on a metal plate. Hooray—free shoes!

The Rules

It sounds very simple: row your boat down a 2,000-meter course in a straight line, faster than your opponents. However, it's a bit more complicated than that.

You and your teammates have to move the oars in and out of the water with perfect timing or the boat will slow down. So you can't stop for a second to scratch your nose.

Steering the boat is usually done by one of the rowers, but bigger boats have a small loud person facing the opposite way sitting at the back, called a coxswain, or cox. They control the rudder and bark orders like "Hurry up—we're losing," and "My dinner is getting cold."

STROKE
This rower sets the timing and rhythm of the oars in the water. They're usually the best rower in the boat, too.

COXSWAIN
A small member of rowing team that shouts directions at the rest of them.

Sound Like a Pro

"SHELL"
Another name for a boat

"ENGINE ROOM"
The middle rowers in a boat, who provide most of the power

"BLADES"
Another name for oars

"SCULL"
To row with an oar in each hand

"SWEEP"
To row with both hands on one oar

BEST EVER:

The USA, Germany, and Great Britain have always been the strongest powerhouses in rowing. The USA has 89 medals, 33 of them gold.

Great Britain's Steven Redgrave has six medals, five of which are gold. While Romanian Elisabeta Lipă has eight medals, including five golds.

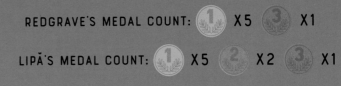

REDGRAVE'S MEDAL COUNT: ① X5 ③ X1

LIPĂ'S MEDAL COUNT: ① X5 ② X2 ③ X1

UPSIDES

Rowing is a great sport for building your fitness and making friends working as a team. You also get to eat loads of food to keep your energy levels up.

DOWNSIDES

Training is hard-core, with early-morning starts in all kinds of weather. Rowers are often so exhausted at the end of a race that they collapse.

SAILING

WHAT IS IT?

Sailors must sail their choice of boat around a course trying to be faster than their opponents, battling the wind and currents.

TWO SAILORS
In most races, there are two sailors: the helmsman, at the tiller (for steering) and working the mainsail, and a crew person working the other sail or sails.

TRAPEZE
Sometimes the crew has to lean right outside the boat to keep the boat steady; they stay attached by a trapeze wire connected to the mast.

MAINSAIL
Boats may have to sail in a zigzag pattern along the course as they maneuver in relation to the wind.

BEST EVER:

Being an island nation, Great Britain really does "rule the waves," as the song goes. They have 58 medals, 28 of them gold.

Great Britain's Ben Ainslie is one of the most successful sailors at the Summer Games, with five medals, four of them gold.

AINSLIE'S MEDAL COUNT: ①X4 ②X1

Sound Like a Pro

"KNOT"
A measure of speed

"STARBOARD"
The right-hand side of the boat

"PORT"
The left-hand side of the boat

"WINDWARD"
The side closest to the wind

"SHEET"
A rope used to control a sail

MARK BUOY
The course is set out with various markers; crews will jostle to sail closest to the mark.

A CLOSER LOOK

BASIC TRAINING

Fold several pieces of paper into a fleet of small boats. Color the sails with flags from countries around the world and then place them in a bathtub filled with water. Get a handheld fan and point it at the bath to create wind. Then watch the boats float around for six hours and try to figure out which boat has won the race.

SKILLS NEEDED

Sailing is very physically and mentally tough. It's not all sitting on the deck having a nice picnic and looking at the sky. Sailors can be competing for six hours a day, physically battling with the sails while mentally processing huge amounts of information about wind speed, currents, clouds, and tides. Intelligence and good seamanship are crucial, especially when the water beneath you is constantly changing.

The Rules

There are roughly ten races in each of the eight different events, although just to be different the 49er class has 15 races. Boats get points for their finishing positions in each race, so you get one point for coming first, two points for coming in second, and so on. Ten boats advance to the medal race, in which points are doubled. The boat with the lowest score wins.

It can be very hard for spectators to tell what's going on, especially if they have forgotten their binoculars.

UPSIDES

Catch the right wind in your sail and you'll be flying along, leaving everyone else behind. It takes a lot of effort to do well in so many races, so you really earn your medal.

DOWNSIDES

It's very hard work and you're on the water for a long period. Sailors tend to be tactically brutal with each other, so you might not make friends here.

A BIT OF HISTORY

Sailing has been around since humans realized that floating on water was better than drowning in it. After that, people continued to use boats for moving things around the world and for fighting. Then someone decided boats could be fun, and sailing joined the Summer Games in 1900. It was canceled in 1904 because there weren't enough boats but rejoined in 1908. It was called yachting until 2000.

INJURIES

Cuts, bruises, and hand injuries from rope burn are common. So is banging your head on the boom of the sail. Don't worry, drowning is extremely rare.

CHANCE OF BECOMING A CHAMPION

Slim | Okay | Good | Great

Sailing is not a cheap sport, and you need to live near a large body of water. If you do have access to a boat, then your chances are much improved.

ATHLETICS
Track Events

WHAT IS IT?

Athletes run around a big oval track as fast as possible and for various distances. To make it slightly trickier, some athletes have to jump over things, while others have to pass a baton.

MIDDLE DISTANCE

TANK TOP
To keep cool, most long-distance runners wear loose-fitting, lightweight sleeveless tops.

LIGHTWEIGHT SHORT SHORTS
Made from a breathable fabric

BASIC TRAINING

Running is one of easiest sports to train for—you have the whole world to jog around.

Sound Like a Pro

"PACEMAKER"
A runner who deliberately sets a fast pace. They usually drop out before the finish and let other team members win.

"DEAD HEAT"
When it's impossible to tell who has won a race and it's called a tie

"ANCHOR LEG"
The last runner in the relay team, usually the fastest

"FALSE START"
Moving before the starting gun has been fired

INJURIES

Legs, hips, knees, groin, ankles, and feet take the most punishment, so make sure you warm up and cool down properly.

A BIT OF HISTORY

Early humans probably invented running while being chased by saber-toothed tigers. However, most of the time the humans weren't quick enough and ended up as dinner. Because running is so simple, it's no surprise that it was one of the sports in the first modern Games, in 1896. Women's events were added in 1928 and included in the first Paralympics, in 1960.

EPIC FAIL

Surinam's 800-meter runner Wim Esajas apparently overslept and missed his one and only heat at the 1960 Olympics. However, it was later discovered he was given the wrong starting time by officials.

HIGH HURDLES
These are L-shaped and designed to fall forward if runners clip them as they jump, which avoids getting their legs in a nasty tangle.

POWERFUL LUNGS
Distance runners need an incredible amount of stamina to keep up a fast and steady pace for a long time.

A CLOSER LOOK

SPIKED RUNNING SHOES
Athletes wear special shoes to absorb the impact of each step, with spikes for added grip.

THE EVENTS

SPRINTING
- 100 meters • 200 meters • 400 meters
- 4 x 100 meters relay • 4 x 400 meters relay

There are the same distances at the Paralympics but with 15 different classifications depending on ability. The 100 meters is the biggest event at every Summer Games, even though it's over in around ten seconds. Sprinters have to have explosive power to sprint very quickly for a very short period of time—45 seconds for 400 meters, which is one whole lap of the track.

HURDLES
- 110 meters (for men) • 100 meters (for women)
- 400 meters (men and women)

Runners must sprint and also clear ten hurdles as fast as possible before the finish line. Hurdles are usually waist height, so it takes some skill to get over them without breaking stride or falling flat on your face.

MIDDLE DISTANCE
- 800 meters (two laps around the track) • 1,500 meters (three and three quarter laps) • 3,000-meter steeplechase (with hurdles and a water pit to jump)

These are more tactical races, with a mixture of jogging and sprinting. Runners bunch up together and are constantly checking over their shoulders to see where their rivals are before they get ready to sprint the last lap.

UPSIDES
Telling everyone you are the fastest person on the planet is impressive, and successful track athletes are some of the most famous people in the world.

DOWNSIDES
Training is hard, and long-distance runners spend a long time away from home. Sprinters can get injured very easily, and coming fourth in a race must be one of the worst feelings ever.

LONG DISTANCE
- 5,000 meters • 10,000 meters • marathon (about 42 kilometers/26 miles around a city)

These events are a true test of stamina, endurance, and mental toughness and another tactical battle with your rivals. Your whole body will be saying "This isn't fun anymore. Can we stop now and sit down?" Long-distance runners are very different from their muscular sprinting teammates—they're usually wiry with hardly any body fat.

BEST EVER

The USA's Carl Lewis has nine golds and one silver, in 100 meters, 200 meters, 4 x 100 meters relay, and the long jump. Jamaica's Usain Bolt has eight golds, in 100 meters, 200 meters, and 4 x 100 meters relay. Maybe he should have done the long jump, too! Bolt is currently the world record holder in 100 meters and 200 meters. So he's the fastest person on the planet!

The USA's Allyson Felix has nine medals, six gold.

Angolan Paralympic sprinter José Sayovo has eight medals (four gold), in 100 meters, 200 meters, and 400 meters.

LEWIS'S MEDAL COUNT: 🥇 X9 🥈 X1

RACE WALKING
- 20 kilometers • 50 kilometers (for men only)

Walking is the sport where everyone looks like they are trying to get to the bathroom as quickly as possible. Athletes must make sure one foot appears to be on the ground at all times. Failure to do this is called a "loss of contact." Three of these and you get a red card and are out. Imagine walking 49 kilometers and getting a red card on your final lap!

ATHLETICS
Field Events

WHAT IS IT?

The throwing and jumping side of athletics, done in the middle of the oval track while everyone is really watching the runners

HIGH JUMP

FOSBURY FLOP
This jumping technique is named after Dick Fosbury, a 1968 high jump champion.

SHOES
To give high jumpers an extra spring in their step, some wear one shoe with tiny spikes on the sole.

HIGH BAR
The bar gets higher and higher as the competition goes on.

A TANK TOP AND SHORTS
Keeping it simple

SOFT LANDING
The pad is usually at least 1 meter (3 feet) thick to cushion the jumper's landing.

A CLOSER LOOK

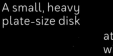

DISCUS
A small, heavy plate-size disk

HAMMER
A metal ball attached to a wire with a grip handle on the end

SHOT
A shot is about the same weight as a bowling ball.

THE EVENTS

TRIPLE JUMP

For athletes who want to make the long jump more fun—add a hop and a skip before jumping into the big sand pit.

LONG JUMP

Sprint down the runway until you reach a white board, then leap forward as far as you can, landing in a sand pit so you don't hurt your bottom. If you step beyond the board, your jump doesn't count.

HIGH JUMP

Jumpers try to leap over a bar without knocking it down. They attempt this by doing a Fosbury flop, which entails leaping headfirst, then arching their back over the bar. All jumpers must take off on one foot. They land on a big pad (or it would really hurt).

POLE VAULT

Pole vaulters sprint down a runway carrying a long pole. When they get to the end, they plant the pole into a box and swing their way up into the air and, they hope, over a very high bar.

Throwers need strength, power, and timing. Jumpers need feet made of springs.

SHOT PUT

CHALK ON THEIR HANDS
Throwers use chalk to keep whatever they're throwing from slipping.

TIGHT LEGGINGS
Since it can get chilly waiting around for your next turn

THROWING CIRCLE
This has a non-slippery surface so throwers don't slip as they're spinning.

A Bit of History

Challenging each other to throw things farther or jump higher than anyone else has been around for thousands of years. Javelin, discus, and long jump were included in the ancient Games. Discus and long jump were in the first modern Games in 1896, with javelin added in 1908.

The 1896 Games also included triple jump, which was probably based on playground hopscotch; high jump, which started in Scotland in the 1800s; pole vault, which began as a way for people to quickly get over rivers and marshes; and shot put, which came from soldiers chucking cannonballs around in the Middle Ages. The hammer throw started in the Middle Ages when people hurled the blacksmith's hammer while he wasn't looking, and joined the Summer Games in 1900.

BASIC TRAINING

It's all about the shouting. First thing in the morning, leap out of bed, stamp both feet and roar like a polar bear with a headache. In the afternoon, when you get home from school, burst through the front door and bellow like a camel with a sore foot. Do this twice. Then in the evening, walk around the house clapping until the rest of your family joins in, then go and leap over the sofa.

Sound Like a Pro

"CAGE"
A high fence around the throwing circle in discus and hammer. This stops the crowd from getting hit in the face if a throw goes wrong.

"IMPACT AREA"
Where the javelin, shot put, discus, and hammer are supposed to land after being thrown. Judges stand here and try not to get hit.

"FLIGHT PHASE"
The time a jumper is in the air

"TAKEOFF BOARD"
Where a triple or long jumper takes off from

JAVELIN

Charge down the runway, carrying a long spear level with your head. Chuck it into the air as high and far as you can. Make sure you don't step over the fault line at the end of the runway or your throw won't count.

SHOT PUT

Start with a metal ball (shot) tucked under your chin and near your neck, then hurl it above shoulder height as far as you can without stepping out of the throwing circle.

DISCUS THROW

Put your hand over the top of your discus, then spin around the throwing circle until you reach top speed and throw. Luckily the discus doesn't smash like a plate would when it hits the ground.

HAMMER THROW

Spin around and around and around and around, then let go, zinging your hammer high into the air as far as it will possibly go. At the Paralympics, athletes throw a wooden club instead.

Athletics
DECATHLON and HEPTATHLON

WHAT IS IT?

A multisport track-and-field event for superhuman competitors out to prove they are the "World's Greatest Athlete"

A CLOSER LOOK

LUCKY UNDERWEAR
Athletes probably change their clothes between events, but they might have a pair of lucky underwear that they like to keep on at all times.

1 SPRINTING (100/200 METERS)
Imagine being chased by an angry cheetah.

THE EVENTS
- SPRINTING (m/w)
- LONG JUMP (m/w)
- SHOT PUT (m/w)
- HIGH JUMP (m/w)
- MIDDLE DISTANCE (m/w)
- HURDLES (m/w)
- DISCUS THROW (m)
- POLE VAULT (m)
- JAVELIN THROW (m/w)
- 1,500 METERS (m)

m = men   w = women

2 LONG JUMP
You'll get lots of sand up your shorts.

3 SHOT PUT
Chucking a heavy metal ball, which leaves an impressive dent in the field

4 HIGH JUMP
This is jumping over a really high bar—basically the opposite of the limbo.

5 MIDDLE DISTANCE (400 M + 800 M)
Imagine being chased by an angry bear.

INJURIES
With so many different events, there are more chances of injuries.

The Rules

Decathlon is for men and is ten events across two days: 100 meters, long jump, shot put, high jump, 400 meters, 110-meter hurdles, discus throw, pole vault, javelin throw, and 1,500 meters.

Heptathlon is for women and is seven events across two days: 100-meter hurdles, high jump, shot put, 200 meters, long jump, javelin throw, and 800 meters.

Athletes score points for how well they perform in each event, and the one with the most points at the end is the winner. They also have to fit in bathroom breaks, eating, and getting advice from their coach in the short breaks between events.

CHANCE OF BECOMING A CHAMPION

| Slim | Okay | Good | Great |

Very slim. You have to be a spectacular athlete to even think about doing the decathlon or heptathlon. Most competitors would have a better chance of winning a medal if they entered one of the single events!

A BIT OF HISTORY

The decathlon and heptathlon can be traced back to the ancient Games—when organizers got so fed up with athletes bragging about how good they were at everything that they invented a five-part event called the pentathlon, with sprint, javelin, discus, long jump, and wrestling.

The 1904 Summer Games featured an all-around event, which became the decathlon in 1912. They quickly dropped the wrestling, though, because nobody liked getting beaten up. Women started a pentathlon in 1964, which became a heptathlon in 1984.

BASIC TRAINING

There is no time for basic training. You must do real training all the time—as soon as you wake up until it gets dark, and even when you're in bed and in your dreams. If you get up to pee during the night, also do ten push-ups.

Sound Like a Pro

"OWWW, THIS REALLY HURTS"

"I WANT MY MOMMY"

"WHAT DO YOU MEAN THERE'S STILL SEVEN EVENTS LEFT?!"

Okay, these aren't special terms—they're what you'd probably be saying to yourself during a competition.

6

HURDLES
Trying to run fast when someone's put lots of little fences in the way

7

DISCUS
Throwing a chunky plate as far as possible

UPSIDES

If you win Olympic gold, you are officially one of the world's greatest athletes.

DOWNSIDES

It is mentally and physically exhausting. Some people call it the toughest sporting event on earth.

8

POLE VAULT
This is basically flying using a really long stick.

10

1,500 METERS
Imagine being chased by an angry duck.

9

JAVELIN
This would be more fun if it were called spear hurling.

SKILLS NEEDED

Everything! Strength, speed, power, great stamina, a spring in your heels . . . the list goes on. Most athletes specialize in a handful of events that will give them maximum points, so they don't have to do that well in others. For example, a good decathlete might do really well in eight events, which should give them enough points to get away with not doing so well in the other two events.

GYMNASTICS

Rings

WHAT IS IT?

Very flexible athletes compete in a series of different events, with amazing acrobatic routines and feats of strength.

THE APPARATUSES

- **BALANCE BEAM** (w)
- **FLOOR** (m/w)
- **HORIZONTAL BAR** (m)
- **PARALLEL BARS** (m)
- **POMMEL HORSE** (m)
- **RINGS** (m)
- **UNEVEN BARS** (w)
- **VAULT** (m/w)

m = men   w = women

INJURIES

Severe injuries are rare, but your ankles, wrists, knees, feet, back, and hands will get a workout—especially with bad landings.

SKILLS NEEDED

You need to be flexible and strong, with a sense of style and, most importantly, courage. Gymnasts are usually small, compact, and powerful. Not many are over six feet.

BASIC TRAINING

Start with a simple handstand. Then walk around doing a handstand, then do a one-hand push-up in a handstand. Now go to the grocery store doing a handstand and do a double backward somersault into the store. See? Gymnastics is simple!

LEOTARDS
Female gymnasts call it a leotard; males prefer to call them singlets or competition shirts. They are tight-fitting so the judges can always see the shape of the gymnast's moves.

CHUNKY WRIST BANDS AND HAND SUPPORTS
To protect themselves from injuries

Sound Like a Pro

"GIANT"
A full rotation of the bar in a handstand position

"RIP"
A blister or wound, usually on the hand or wrist

"MOUNT" or **"DISMOUNT"**
To get on or off an apparatus

"STICK A LANDING"
To make a perfect landing

"SALTO"
Fancy name for a flip or somersault

BEST EVER

The Soviet Union (now Russia) is home to the best artistic gymnastics, with 182 medals, 72 of which are gold. The USA is next, with 114, then Japan, with 98.

Russia's Larisa Latynina holds the record for most gymnastic medals, with 18, nine of those gold. She is the most successful female athlete in any sport, and second only to US swimmer Michael Phelps in the all-time most medals list.

CHANCE OF BECOMING A CHAMPION

Slim	Okay	Good	Great

You need to be super bendy and strong to even climb on most of the apparatuses. Gymnasts are usually selected at a very young age.

LATYNINA'S MEDAL COUNT: ①X9 ②X5 ③X4

A BIT OF HISTORY

Gymnastics can be traced back to ancient Greece, where soldiers used gymnastic moves to get ready for war. They did all this with no clothes on, only stopping to get dressed when it was time to battle. In the 1700s, gymnastic apparatuses were invented and were first used by the military, schools, and sports clubs.

Artistic gymnastics became one of the first sports to appear at the modern Games in 1896, with a women's team event joining in 1928. A full roster of women's events arrived a bit later, in 1952.

UPSIDES

It's easy to impress someone if you can do a flying double somersault.

DOWNSIDES

Training is long and hard. You need to be incredibly committed to learn skills on all the different apparatuses.

BALANCE BEAM (WOMEN)

Gymnasts perform a routine of jumps, leaps, and flips on a thin wooden beam no wider than their feet.

FLOOR (MEN AND WOMEN)

A routine on a big mat, usually with lots of flying somersaults

HORIZONTAL BAR (MEN)

Athletes swing, flip, and twist themselves around a bar, sometimes flying into the air and hoping to catch the bar on the way down.

PARALLEL BARS (MEN)

Gymnasts swing, balance, and lift themselves using two high bars that are next to each other. Call them p-bars to sound cool.

POMMEL HORSE (MEN)

A headless, tailless horse, with two handles (pommels) in the middle. Gymnasts swing their legs around the horse and support the rest of their body with their hands.

RINGS (MEN)

Gymnasts perform muscle-crunching moves while clinging on to two high rings hanging from a metal frame. Super strength is needed—it's the gymnastics version of weightlifting.

UNEVEN BARS (WOMEN)

Two bars at different heights, which gymnasts swing between and perform tricks from

VAULT (MEN AND WOMEN)

Gymnasts sprint down a runway, leap off a springboard, and throw themselves toward the vault to perform a midair pirouette or something equally amazing. Then they have to land perfectly on the other side.

A CLOSER LOOK

CHALK
To help with grip and keep the gymnasts' hands from getting sweaty

BARE FEET, SOCKS, OR SOFT SHOES
Footwear varies by event.

Pommel Horse

LEGGINGS WITH STIRRUPS
The stirrups are loops around the bottom of the feet to keep the pant legs from riding up.

SPARKLE
Female athletes' makeup, hair, and leotards get the full treatment. This hasn't spread to the men's event yet.

Balance Beam

GYMNASTICS
Trampoline

WHAT IS IT?

The closest an athlete will get to flying, with a few bouncy, acrobatic tricks thrown in.

The Rules

Athletes get ten bounces to perform a series of acrobatic tricks, somersaults, twists, and other crazy moves. Judges award points for difficulty, execution, and flight time (there are actually points for flying!). You lose points for failing to do a trick, falling, or landing badly. Whoever has the most points at the end is the winner.

LEOTARDS
Trampoliners wear the same uniforms as other gymnasts. Some men may wear a tank top and tight-fitting pants.

BASIC TRAINING

Just jump up and down on your parents' bed. When they come in to tell you to stop, leap over their heads with a flying somersault and run away.

Sound Like a Pro

"BED"
This is the part of the trampoline you jump on.

"KILLER"
A double back somersault with four twists

"FLIFFUS"
A double somersault with at least a half twist

"SPOTTER"
The person who makes sure you don't fall off

A BIT OF HISTORY

Today's trampoline wasn't invented until 1935, and it was first used to train astronauts! Trampolining wasn't added to the Summer Games until 2000.

INJURIES

All over—arms, legs, neck, and face. Landing badly on any of these body parts is going to leave a big bruise.

A BIG RECTANGULAR TRAMPOLINE
It's usually about 5 meters (16 ½ feet) long by 3 meters (10 feet) wide, so it's pretty different from the little round ones in people's backyards.

BIG PADS AND MATS
In case you fall off

RED CROSS
This marks the center of the jumping zone.

SKILLS NEEDED

You need to be able to twist your body into the shape of a pretzel. It also helps if you have a head for heights, as you could go as high as 10 meters (33 feet)—that's about three elephants standing on top of one another!

UPSIDES

Unless you are planning on growing wings, this is your best chance to fly.

DOWNSIDES

It can get very messy if you get your trick or bounce wrong and you end up flying through the air out of control.

RHYTHMIC

WHAT IS IT?

Female gymnasts perform ballet moves, leaps, tumbles, pirouettes, and other fancy gymnastic tricks while using an assortment of props.

THE APPARATUSES

- RIBBON
- CLUB
- HOOP
- BALL

The Rules

For the individual event, gymnasts perform once with each prop, called an apparatus. In the team event, five gymnasts perform twice using different props at the same time. Judges award points for how difficult the moves and tricks are, how well they are done, and how aesthetically pleasing the routine is. The highest score wins.

A LONG RIBBON ATTACHED TO A SHORT STICK

The gymnast flicks, circles, spirals, and snakes the ribbon and, to make it really hard, throws the stick into the air.

A LEOTARD COVERED IN TWINKLY BITS

For a bit of sparkle, glitz, and glamour

BASIC TRAINING

Start with the ribbon since it looks like the easiest (but probably isn't). Flick it repeatedly at your dad while he's trying to watch television. When he chases you out of the room, leave a club, a ball, and a hoop by the door so he trips over them.

Sound Like a Pro

"ARABESQUE"

Standing on one leg with the other in the air at a 90-degree angle

"AERIAL CARTWHEEL"

A cartwheel without your hands touching the floor

"SPLIT LEAP"

A split in midair

SLIPPERS

Special half-shoes that cover only the front of the foot

A CLOSER LOOK

A LARGE PLASTIC OR WOODEN HOOP

For swinging, throwing, catching, and leaping through

A RUBBER BALL

About the size of your head. It's thrown, caught, bounced, and rolled.

SOFTISH CLUBS, A BIT LIKE BOWLING PINS

For spinning, throwing, and catching. Sadly, they are not set on fire. You lose points for drops.

A Bit of History

In the olden days, emperors, kings, and evil warlords watched acrobats perform and usually killed the ones they didn't like. This went on for hundreds of years, until the 1800s, when it turned into a version of rhythmic gymnastics and nobody got killed. The Russians turned it into a sport in the 1940s, because they were really good at it, and it became competitive in the 1960s. Rhythmic gymnastics joined the Summer Games in 1984, and the team part was added in 1996.

SKILLS NEEDED

You need to be flexible, agile, and coordinated and have a sense of style and grace. This probably isn't for you if you're clumsy.

UPSIDES

It's very popular with the crowds because it's exciting to watch the amazing routines.

DOWNSIDES

A lot of long training sessions that make your body feel like it might snap in half.

CHANCE OF BECOMING A CHAMPION

| Slim | Okay | Good | Great |

If you've been dancing since you could walk, then you might have a chance.

Sport Climbing

WHAT IS IT?

Being higher up than everyone else is one of the great things about being an astronaut, mountaineer, stilt walker, very tall person — or a sport climber.

The Rules

This version of sport climbing comprises three events:
1) Speed climbing, in which two climbers race against each other up a 15-meter wall
2) Bouldering, in which each climber scales a course on a 4-meter wall in a fixed time
3) Lead climbing, in which competitors try to climb the highest in a fixed time
The best person at all three events will win gold.

BASIC TRAINING

It all starts with a bunk bed. Don't use the ladder, practice climbing to the top bunk and note down your fastest time. If you don't have a bunk bed, find a tree. But be very careful: trees don't come with mattresses to fall on if you make a mistake.

A CLOSER LOOK

A SAFETY ROPE
Usually made of nylon, it needs to be strong and flexible.

BEST EVER

The first sport climbing medals are being awarded at the 2020 Summer Games, when the sport makes its debut.

NEAR-VERTICAL WALL
Since it's hard to move a mountain and put it into an arena, climbers have to use a very high wall instead.

BRIGHTLY COLORED HANDHOLDS, FINGERHOLDS, AND FOOTHOLDS
Holds help competitors climb up the wall and enable them to plan their route.

BARE HANDS ONLY
Climbers aren't allowed to wear gloves and need to make sure they've trimmed their fingernails.

CHALK
Keeps climbers' hands dry and helps with grip.

EXTREMELY TIGHT, SOFT SHOES
These help climbers' feet grip the wall.

SKILLS NEEDED

You need to be strong, agile, and flexible and have fingertips made of iron, as well as a powerful grip. You also need a strategic brain to plan your route carefully. It's no good being fast if you find yourself climbing onto the roof of the supermarket by mistake.

Sound Like a Pro

"GUMBY"
An inexperienced climber

"BETA"
Information on how to complete a climbing route

"FLATLANDER"
A nonclimber

"CRUX"
The hardest part of a climb

"FLASH"
To complete a route on the first attempt

"PEEL"
To fall

"BI-DOIGT"
(bee-dwah)
A climbing hold big enough for just two fingers

"CUT-LOOSE"
When a climber is hanging by just their hands

CHALK BAG
Unfortunately, this pouch is not for tasty snacks on the way up—just for chalk (which tastes, well, like chalk).

UPSIDES

Climbing to the top faster than anyone else is a huge thrill and a great confidence boost. Once you've climbed to the top of a high wall or mountain, you feel like you can do anything.

DOWNSIDES

It can be very painful. You'll sometimes have to hold your whole body weight with just two fingers.

INJURIES

Sore fingers and scraped knees are common, but more serious injuries are usually in the shoulders because they do most of the work. The safety ropes prevent most serious injuries.

A Bit of History

Early humans probably started climbing to avoid being eaten by saber-toothed tigers thousands of years ago, but climbing has had to wait until 2020 to make its first appearance at the Summer Games. Sadly, the saber-toothed tiger has been replaced by a stopwatch.

CHANCE OF BECOMING A CHAMPION

Slim	Okay	Good	Great

Most top climbers specialize in just one of the events, so if you can master all three, you've got a great chance.

TRIATHLON

WHAT IS IT?

Three long-distance sports in one—swimming, cycling, and running—with no breaks

The Rules

The Summer Games triathlon starts with a swim of 1,500 meters, usually in a lake, a river, or the ocean. Then comes a 40-kilometer cycle and a 10-kilometer run. Everyone goes at the same time and the first person to cross the line wins.

WETSUIT
Right after the swim, wriggle out of your wetsuit and throw your goggles off.

1

SWIM CAP
So people can see your head while you're in the water

SHORTS AND VEST IN ONE
Your tri-suit, which you wear underneath your wetsuit, can dry as you cycle.

HELMET AND SUNGLASSES
Put these on as you try to clip your feet into bike pedals and cycle off.

2

Sound Like a Pro

"BONK"
To lose your energy

"BOPER"
Someone who is at the back of the pack

"FRED"
Someone who has lots of fancy gear but hardly ever uses it

"CD"
Cool down

CHANCE OF BECOMING A CHAMPION

Slim   Okay   Good   ↑   Great

Triathlon is growing around the world, and there are also more places up for grabs at the Olympics with a new mixed relay event, in which teams of two men and two women will do a 300-meter swim, an 8-kilometer cycle, and a 2-kilometer run.

A Bit of History

Bored with running, some Americans decided to throw some more sports into their daily workout and then put together the first modern triathlon in California in the mid-1970s.

Triathlon became incredibly popular and joined the Summer Games in 2000 and the Paralympics in 2016.

3

SOCKS
It will slow you down to put these on, but they prevent blisters.

LOCK LACES
Elastic shoelaces that you don't have to tie up, to save time

UPSIDES

People are impressed if you say you've done a triathlon because they are very tough.

DOWNSIDES

Triathlon is THE "getting changed into different clothes and swapping equipment" sport. Unfortunately, you must do it all mid-race. If it takes you a long time to get dressed, this isn't the sport for you.

MODERN PENTATHLON

WHAT IS IT?

Five different sports—fencing, swimming, riding, shooting, and running—packed into one day. A true test of all-around sporting ability.

Unusually, Hungary and Sweden top the medal charts, with nine golds each. Hungarian András Balczó has three golds and two silvers.

THE EVENTS
- FENCING
- RIDING
- RUNNING
- SHOOTING
- SWIMMING

SKILLS NEEDED

Everything! Apart from mountain climbing and cooking skills.

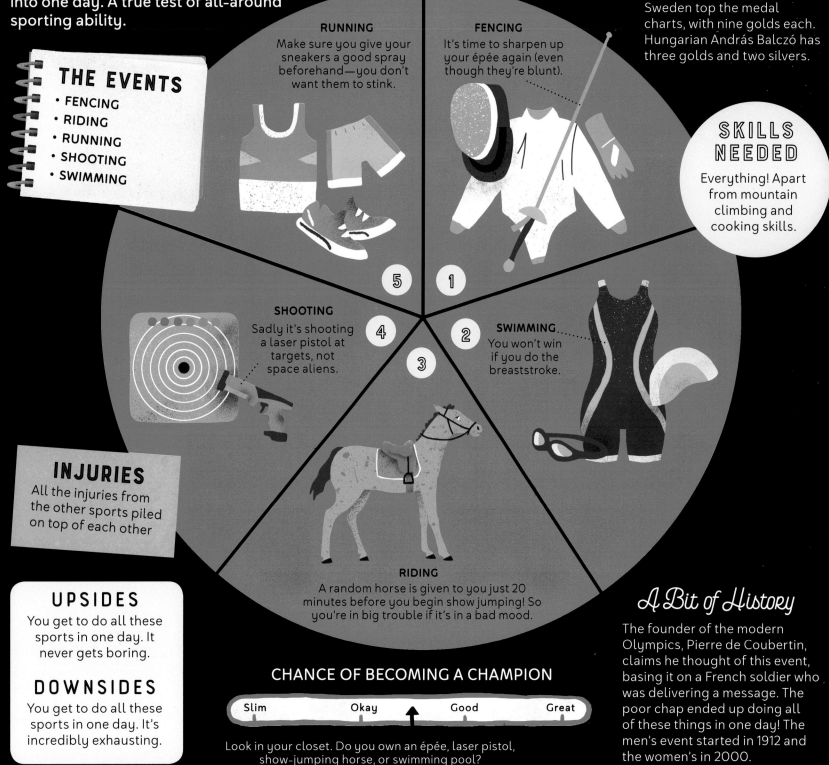

RUNNING
Make sure you give your sneakers a good spray beforehand—you don't want them to stink.

FENCING
It's time to sharpen up your épée again (even though they're blunt).

SHOOTING
Sadly it's shooting a laser pistol at targets, not space aliens.

SWIMMING
You won't win if you do the breaststroke.

RIDING
A random horse is given to you just 20 minutes before you begin show jumping! So you're in big trouble if it's in a bad mood.

INJURIES
All the injuries from the other sports piled on top of each other

UPSIDES
You get to do all these sports in one day. It never gets boring.

DOWNSIDES
You get to do all these sports in one day. It's incredibly exhausting.

CHANCE OF BECOMING A CHAMPION

Slim	Okay	Good	Great

Look in your closet. Do you own an épée, laser pistol, show-jumping horse, or swimming pool?

A Bit of History

The founder of the modern Olympics, Pierre de Coubertin, claims he thought of this event, basing it on a French soldier who was delivering a message. The poor chap ended up doing all of these things in one day! The men's event started in 1912 and the women's in 2000.

WEIGHTLIFTING

WHAT IS IT?

Athletes lift heavy weights attached to a bar, then stand as still as possible for a few seconds.

SKILLS NEEDED

Explosive power and strength. If you struggle to lift a heavy suitcase, this sport isn't for you. You can be any shape and size to be a top weightlifter. Competitors are put in different categories depending on their body weight.

The Rules

Weightlifters compete in two disciplines at the Summer Games: "clean and jerk," which sounds like washing up while breakdancing but isn't, and the "snatch," which sadly isn't about stealing candy.

In a snatch, the weights are lifted in one motion. In clean and jerk, it's two movements: up to the shoulders (the clean), then above the head (the jerk). Lifters have to the hold the weights in position above their head with their arms and legs in a straight lock until a buzzer tells them it's time to stop.

Competitors have three tries to lift each weight, and if they're successful, the weight is increased.

FINGER AND KNEE TAPE
Weightlifters cover their fingers, thumbs, wrists, and knees in tape to help prevent injuries.

CHALK
LIfters rub chalk all over their hands to keep the bar from slipping.

SINGLET
Sometimes worn with a T-shirt underneath

WEIGHT PLATES
Sometimes called bumper plates, they are covered in rubber so they can be dropped from a height without smashing through the floor.

MASSIVE BELT
Weightlifting belts support and stabilize the lifter's spine.

A CLOSER LOOK

BARBELL
The bumper plates attach to a steel bar.

BASIC TRAINING

Cover yourself in chalk, then get a stick and hang an increasing number of heavy things on the ends. Lift the stick above your head and let out a bloodcurdling scream to make it clear that what you're doing is incredibly tough. Make sure you don't lift the heaviest thing right away or you'll hurt yourself.

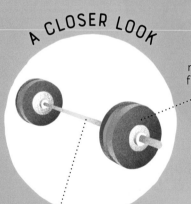

FINAL PUSH
The final position of the lift, with straight legs and the weights above the head

COLOR-CODED WEIGHTS
Different weights are different colors — simple!

GURNING
Weightlifters make all kinds of unusual faces when lifting. Sometimes it looks like their heads are about to pop off their shoulders.

SHOES WITH A RAISED HEEL
They help the weightlifter squat deeper to generate more power.

KNEES ON DISPLAY
Judges need to be able to see knees and elbows at all times.

INJURIES
Lifters' knees, wrists, and shoulders take a battering, but nasty injuries are rare unless they get their technique all wrong.

Sound Like a Pro

"HANG"
The starting position when the weight is lifted off the floor — and usually the moment the lifter realizes they made a big mistake

"COLLARS"
The fittings at the end of the barbell that keep the weights from sliding off

"KNURLING"
The grip texture on a barbell

BEST EVER

The Soviet Union, China, and the United States top the medal charts, but special mention to Bulgaria, which does well. It's Bulgaria's second-best sport after wrestling.

Pyrros Dimas is the best Olympic weightlifter, with three golds and one bronze, and is Greece's best-ever competitor. He is nicknamed Midas and began weightlifting at age 11.

DIMAS'S MEDAL COUNT: ① X3 ③ X1

CHANCE OF BECOMING A CHAMPION

Slim   Okay   Good   ↑ Great

Lifting weights is very popular in the gym, but the sport requires different skills and not as many people compete.

UPSIDES
You'll be one of the strongest people in the world, plus you can eat a ton of food. Weightlifters sometimes eat 8,000 calories a day — four times the usual amount!

DOWNSIDES
It's painful and repetitive and can make your muscles really sore.

A Bit of History

People in prehistoric times used to lift heavy rocks to see who was the strongest. Modern-style weightlifting took off in the eighteenth and nineteenth centuries, when strongmen performed at the circus. It was so popular that it became one of the first sports in the modern Games. Women's weightlifting joined the Games in 2000.

Badminton

WHAT IS IT?

A racket sport that involves hitting a shuttlecock over a high net. It's very fast and very squeaky.

BASIC TRAINING

Badminton is the perfect backyard sport as it's almost impossible to smash a window or ping the shuttlecock into your neighbor's yard. You don't even really need a net to get started; a clothesline will do. However, unless one of your family wants to be an umpire, be prepared for lots of arguments: "That was in!" "No, it wasn't!" "Yes, it was!" and so on.

A Bit of History

Badminton was originally played in India in the 1800s as poona. British soldiers took the game back home, and in 1873 a British duke renamed it after his country house, Badminton. It's lucky the house wasn't called Cow's Bottom. Cow's Bottom—er, badminton didn't become an Olympic sport until 1992.

The Rules

Badminton is very simple: hit the shuttlecock over the net and try to get it to land inside the court. If the shuttlecock touches the ground before your opponent gets to it, you win a point. The first to 21 points wins the game, and the best of three games wins the match.

RACKET STRINGS
Called catgut, because they used to be made from animal intestines

VERY LIGHT RACKET
Usually made from carbon fiber

JUMP SMASH
A player can get huge power and an excellent downward angle from this shot.

SQUEAKIEST SNEAKERS YOU'VE EVER HEARD
When badminton is played inside on a shiny floor, the players' sneakers sound like a mouse choir.

A CLOSER LOOK

SHUTTLECOCK
Made from 16 overlapping feathers. The fastest recorded shuttlecock speed in a competition is 265 miles (426 kilometers) per hour!

CHANCE OF BECOMING A CHAMPION

Slim | Okay | Good | Great

Badminton is the second most popular sport worldwide after soccer, with 220 million players. Over a billion people watched badminton at the Barcelona Summer Games in 1992.

SKILLS NEEDED

You will need very bendy wrists, as you'll be playing a lot of shots from strange positions.

BEST EVER

China's Gao Ling is the most decorated Summer Games badminton competitor. She has four medals, two of them gold. China has won 41 badminton medals in total, followed by Indonesia and South Korea.

GAO'S MEDAL COUNT: ① X2 ② X1 ③ X1

UPSIDES

It's the fastest racket sport and is very easy to pick up and play. Smashes are incredibly satisfying, too.

DOWNSIDES

People who don't play sometimes think it's a bit of a plinky-plonky game, and the squeaky-shoe mouse choir can get a bit annoying.

NET
The net is 1.55 meters (5 feet) high, which makes it very hard to jump over if you want to do a fancy winning celebration.

Sound Like a Pro

"PATTY-CAKES"
A rally in which two players hit the shuttlecock back and forth without really moving

"AIR SHOT"
An attempt to hit the shuttlecock that totally misses, swiping at fresh air instead

"BIRD"
Another name for the shuttlecock

"CLEAR"
A high, deep shot to the back of the court

"KILL"
A fast shot that can't be returned

Epic Fail

At the 2012 Summer Games, four women's doubles teams—two South Korean, one Chinese, and one Indonesian— were disqualified for losing their matches on purpose in order to be paired with weaker opponents in the next round.

TENNIS

WHAT IS IT?

A racket sport in which players try to hit a furry bright-yellow ball over a net using a string-covered oval on a stick

A BIT OF HISTORY

Tennis originated with an eleventh-century French handball game called *jeu de paume*. Wooden rackets appeared when the rules of modern tennis were invented in the 1800s, and the game first appeared in the Summer Games in 1896. It was dropped after 1924 and returned in 1988, when tennis players had stopped wearing suits and long dresses to play.

SNEAKERS, SHORTS OR A SKIRT, AND A TOP
White is the most popular color.

BALL BOYS AND BALL GIRLS
Teenagers are plucked from local schools to collect all the balls during a match. It's better than math class.

The Rules

Players try to score points by whacking the ball into their opponent's side of the court and hoping it doesn't come back. Tennis can be played by two players (singles) or four players (doubles), and there are also wheelchair events at the Paralympics.

The tennis scoring system has thrown normal counting out the window. Zero points is called love. The first point you win is 15, the next point is 30, and the next point is 40! Then you win the game. If your opponent levels the score at 40–40, it's called deuce and the next point is called advantage.

The first player to win six games wins a set. The first to win best of three sets is the winner, except in the men's final, where it's best of five sets. You might need to play a few times to get the hang of it.

UPSIDES

Top tennis players are some of the most famous and well-paid sports stars in the world. It's a fun workout, and there are minimal injuries. You can easily play until you are really old—like 42!

DOWNSIDES

It can be hard to get out of a losing spiral. Losing 6–0, 6–0, 6–0 (a triple bagel!) is no fun. Some tennis players lose their temper—with themselves, the umpire, and their rackets.

BASIC TRAINING

Let's go back to *jeu de paume* for this bit of basic training. Grab a ball of any size, stand by a wall, and throw the ball against it. When the ball comes back, smack it at the wall with the palm of your hand. Keep returning the ball to the wall with your hand until you miss. Just be aware—the wall always wins.

Sound Like a Pro

"ACE"
A serve so good that your opponent gets nowhere near it

"GRUNT"
The noise some players make when hitting a ball

"SMASH"
A powerful overhead shot

"BAGEL"
Winning or losing a set 6–0

"SLICE"
A shot with backspin

| Slim | Okay | Good | Great |

With enough dedication and training, becoming a top player is not as hard as it seems. Lots of parks have free tennis courts to practice in. You just need some balls and a racket.

UMPIRE
Sits in a high chair beside the court. He doesn't wear a bib.

NET
Don't hit the ball into the net, or you lose the point. Some players hurdle it when they win.

A CLOSER LOOK

LOTS OF BALLS
You only actually need one, but professional tennis players spend a lot of time studying them, then throwing them away until they find the one they like the look of.

TENNIS RACKET
The most important piece of equipment—made from a lightweight metal with strings sometimes made from animal guts.

TENNIS BALL
Around 300 million tennis balls are produced each year.

INJURIES

Tennis is a very safe sport, and most injuries are muscle-related from overstretching or not warming up enough.

SKILLS NEEDED

Players need to be agile and fit to run around a large court, and skilled in different shots, from lobs to backhand returns. A powerful fast serve is also very handy.

Tennis is a tough mental workout, too. The best players can be staring at defeat one minute, then battling back to victory the next.

Finally, you should be able to let out a loud grunt when hitting the ball.

BEST EVER

The USA and Great Britain dominate the tennis medal table, with 39 and 43 medals respectively. The USA has more gold, with 21.

The USA's Venus Williams is the queen of Olympic tennis, with four golds and one silver. Her sister, Serena, is just behind her, with four golds.

VENUS WILLIAMS'S MEDAL COUNT: X4 ② X1

Table Tennis

WHAT IS IT?

A paddle-and-ball sport that involves hitting a small, light white ball over a tiny net across a table at ferocious speed

The Rules

Serve the ball to your opponent's side of the table and hit it back and forth over the net until someone misses or hits it into the net. The first to 11 points, and at least two points clear, wins the game. A match is best of seven games for singles and the best of five games for doubles.

CHO
Some players shout "cho" after they've won a good point, to pump themselves up. But too much "cho-ing" can be considered rude.

PADDLE
Can also be called a bat or a racket

A CLOSER LOOK

SMALL PLASTIC BALL
The ball is white or orange and light as a feather — almost!

NET
Straight and tight

UPSIDES

Table tennis smash rallies are mesmerizing to watch and can go on for ages. The crowd gets louder and louder with every shot.

DOWNSIDES

The game goes so fast that a really good player can crush you very quickly.

A Bit of History

Table tennis was invented as an after-dinner game by rich English people in the 1880s. They set up play on their large dining tables, using books, cigar box lids, and a champagne cork to create a mini tabletop version of tennis. It was originally called ping-pong, whiff-whaff, or flim-flam, with the term Ping-Pong becoming a trade name.

Despite its popularity around the world, it took until 1988 for table tennis to make it into the Games. However, it's been at the Paralympics since the very start, in 1960.

SQUEAKY SNEAKS
Extra grippy sneakers squeak as players make sharp turns and moves.

TABLE TENNIS GRIPS

There are lots of different ways to hold the table tennis paddle, but the most common fall into two categories: the shakehand and the penhold, which look like they sound.

Front

Back

SHAKEHAND
Like shaking someone's hand; also known as the orthodox grip

Front

Back

PENHOLD
Like holding a pen, with the handle between thumb and forefinger

Sound Like a Pro

"KILL SHOT"
A shot that wins the point

"LOOP"
An aggressive stroke that generates the most topspin

"TWO-WINGED LOOPER"
A player who can play the loop shot well with both forehand and backhand

"PIMPLES" or "PIPS"
The bobbly side of the table tennis paddle, which increases spin on the ball

"TWIDDLING"
Twirling your paddle around to confuse your opponent about which side of the paddle you are going to use

DARK-COLORED TABLE
So the ball stands out

BASIC TRAINING
Push your kitchen table up against a wall, then fire a Ping-Pong ball at it and try to return it using the back of a frying pan.

BEST EVER
China dominates table tennis with 53 medals, 28 of them gold; their total represents half of all the table tennis medals handed out. The next best is South Korea, with just 18. Wang Nan of China is the most successful table tennis player ever in the Summer Games. She has four golds and one silver. She just beats out Deng Yaping, who has four gold medals and is still regarded as one of the greatest players of all time, even though she retired at age 24!

WANG'S MEDAL COUNT: 🥇 X4 🥈 X1

SKILLS NEEDED
You need to be agile and quick on your feet, with great concentration levels and excellent hand-eye coordination. Table tennis is extremely fast — blink and you'll miss it.

CHANCE OF BECOMING A CHAMPION

Slim	Okay	Good	Great

Table tennis is one of China's national sports, and children as young as five can be sent to special table tennis schools if they show early talent. To get the gold, you'll need to be better than about 300 million Chinese players.

CYCLING

Track

HELMET
Special pointy helmets help cyclists cut through the air.

A CLOSER LOOK

The Rules

There are various short sprints and longer endurance races, including strangely named things like keirin, pursuit, madison, and omnium. They all involve chasing each other around a 250-meter oval track, trying to cross the finish line first. Keirin involves a person riding a little motorbike in front of the cyclists to set the pace.

WHAT IS IT?

Racing bikes around a large indoor oval track called a velodrome while constantly looking over your shoulder to see where everyone else is

CYCLING SKINSUIT
With extra padding on the bottom

A BIT OF HISTORY

Cycling on an indoor track started in the late nineteenth century. It was included in the Summer Games in 1896 for men and 1988 for women.

TRACK BIKE
These are fast and light and have carbon wheels. They don't have gears or brakes.

Road

WHAT IS IT?

A very long bike ride on regular roads to see who is the fastest

A Bit of History

Bicycles have been around since the nineteenth century, but it took inventors a few years to add the pedals and stop making the front wheel massive and the back wheel tiny, as in the penny-farthing. People started racing on bikes with rubber tires in the 1860s, and road cycling was one of the few sports to be present at the first modern Summer Games in 1896.

The Rules

Road cycling is very simple: the first to cross the line wins. The race features teams of riders, and teammates work together to help their leader win.

In the time trials, cyclists leave one by one every 90 seconds but still have to complete the course in the fastest time possible. They are racing the clock.

TEAM JERSEY
With a special pocket on the back to carry tasty food supplies

PIT STOP
Cyclists ride for a long time. Some stop to pee behind a tree; some just go while cycling!

CHANCE OF BECOMING A CHAMPION

| Slim | Okay | Good | Great |

Low. There are limited places in cycling teams and cycling is popular all over the world, so you need to be really good.

LONG LINE OF RIDERS

When in a team, event cyclists line up behind one another; it can look like an engine train with cars attached.

Sound Like a Pro

"FIXIE"
A fixed-gear bike with no brakes

"DRAFTING"
When a group of cyclists ride in a line, which helps riders to save energy

"DROPS"
The lower part of curved handlebars

"STEED"
Another name for a bike

BEST EVER

British medalists include some of the greatest cyclists of all time: Bradley Wiggins not only has the most cycling medals (with eight total) but is also Great Britain's most decorated Olympian. Laura Kenny has four gold medals and is the most successful female British Olympian ever.

WIGGINS'S MEDAL COUNT:
① X5   ② X1   ③ X2

UPSIDES
Your legs will look like tree trunks.

DOWNSIDES
You'll spend most of the time looking at someone else's bottom!

SHOES CONNECTED TO THE PEDALS
Cyclists must keep pedaling until the bike slows down and eventually stops.

BASIC TRAINING

Put on clothes that are a bit too tight, then sit on the arm of your sofa in a crouched position and pedal your legs around and around for about six hours.

INJURIES
Some cyclists have gone over the edge of a cliff, but this is very rare.

HELMET
Lightweight and full of holes

Sound Like a Pro

"ATTACK"
An attempt to pull away from the rest of the cyclists

"PELOTON"
The largest group of riders in a race

"RED LANTERN"
The cyclist in last place

"BACON"
Cuts, scabs, scars, and scrapes

"LID"
Another name for a helmet

FINGERLESS GLOVES
To cushion vibrations from the bumpy road

SKILLS NEEDED
You'll need strong, powerful legs; incredible stamina; strategic thinking; and the ability to cycle without toppling over.

SMOOTH LEGS
Riders shave their legs so it's easier to clean scrapes.

ROAD BIKE
Strong but light, with very thin wheels

CYCLING
Mountain Bike

WHAT IS IT?

A long bike race up, down, and across lots of different rough terrains like mud, rocks, streams, and mountains

BREATHABLE CLOTHING
You will get sweaty!

PUNCTURE REPAIR KIT
Mountain bikers must do all their own repairs during the race.

MOUNTAIN BIKE
These are lightweight, with brakes, suspension, and gears.

SHOES
These clip into the pedals to help generate extra power.

A CLOSER LOOK

FAT TIRES
Thick, knobby tires for added grip

Sound Like a Pro

"GNARLY"
Used to describe a difficult part of the course

"ROOST"
Dirt kicked up from a sharp turn

"SNAKE BITE"
A puncture with two holes next to each other

"PINNED"
To be going fast

BEST EVER

France's **Julien Absalon** and Italy's **Paola Pezzo** have two gold medals each.

ABSALON'S AND PEZZO'S MEDAL COUNTS: X 2

INJURIES

Going too fast on uneven ground is dangerous and most falls can lead to cuts and bruises, but shoulder, wrist, and arm injuries are the most common.

A BIT OF HISTORY

People started riding their bikes off-road in the 1800s, when they realized that going on a road wasn't always the quickest way. This led to lots of punctures and broken chains, so specialized mountain bikes started being built in the 1970s. Mountain bike racing pedaled its way into the Summer Games in 1996.

UPSIDES
You get a really good workout in the great outdoors.

DOWNSIDES
The great outdoors can sometimes bite.

The Rules

Around 30 to 50 riders cycle a number of laps around a cross-country course. It usually takes about an hour and a half to finish, and the first person to cross the finish line wins gold.

SKILLS NEEDED

You'll need to enjoy pedaling up hills and getting splattered with mud.

CHANCE OF BECOMING A CHAMPION

Slim — Okay — Good — Great

Low. There are only up to 50 spots in a race, so you really need to be one of the best mountain bikers in the world to be picked. Living near a mountain will help.

BASIC TRAINING

Find a really dense forest and try to bike through it.

BMX

WHAT IS IT?

BMX bike racing is done on a bumpy track with lots of obstacles, jumps, and tight bends. BMX freestyle is the stunt event, which is full of amazing tricks.

A BIT OF HISTORY

BMX started in the United States in the 1960s and was based on motocross—track racing with motorbikes. It became an official Olympic sport in 2008. Freestyle started in the 1970s and joins the Summer Games in 2020.

The Rules

BMX racing entails a series of knockout races among sets of eight athletes, until the roster is whittled down to the final eight racers. Racetracks are usually 300 to 400 meters long, and races last less than a minute. Cross the finish line first to win — simple.

In freestyle, riders take turns doing a series of gravity-defying tricks over jumps, ramps, curbs, walls, and rails. Judges mark riders on two one-minute runs with a score of 0 to 100.

CHANCE OF BECOMING A CHAMPION

Slim   Okay   Good   ↑ Great

Very good. BMX is a very young sport, and your main competitors are teenagers or really old people in their 20s!

A CLOSER LOOK

FULL-FACE HELMET
With mouth guard attached

ELBOW AND KNEE PADS
Built into their clothing

BMX BIKE
A small lightweight bike with just a back brake

Sound Like a Pro

"EAT IT"
To crash hard or fail terribly

"BUTCHER"
A rider who is constantly breaking bits of their bike

"BARSPIN"
A trick where a rider spins the handlebars around in midair

"TRUCK DRIVER"
A trick in which the rider spins the bike 360 degrees in midair while doing a barspin

ROLLERS
A set of dirt mounds placed very close together

INJURIES

The bigger the trick, the nastier the injury.

SKILLS NEEDED

For BMX racing, you need to be strong, with powerful legs for pedaling extra fast around the track. Freestylers need a tremendous amount of skill and nerves of steel.

UPSIDES

Pulling off an amazing trick looks and feels fantastic.

DOWNSIDES

Crashing or messing up a big trick can be frustrating — and painful.

BEST EVER

Latvia's Māris Štrombergs has two golds in men's BMX racing, while Colombia's Mariana Pajón has two golds in women's BMX. They are each the first person from their country ever to win two golds in any sport!

ŠTROMBERGS'S AND PAJÓN'S MEDAL COUNTS: 🥇 X 2

BASIC TRAINING

Find an empty field and ride as fast as possible over any muddy hills.

Equestrian

A CLOSER LOOK

Sound Like a Pro
"NEIGGHHHH"
When's lunch?

WHAT IS IT?
An event featuring the only animal in the Summer Games—a horse. Unlike most other sports, men and women compete against each other.

EVENTING

ALL THE EQUIPMENT
Riders wear a helmet, breeches, boots, and a body protector so they don't hurt themselves if they fall.

HORSES
Not just any old horse—they need to be bold, careful, athletic, and a strong partner with the rider.

WHITE LEG GREASE
In cross-country, some horses have white leg grease to help them slide over the fences.

BASIC TRAINING
Wear your fanciest clothes and go find a huge pile of horse poop to clean up. Try not to get any on your pants or boots.

INJURIES
If you're unlucky enough to be sent crashing to the ground, you risk broken bones, dislocations, and concussions.

The Rules
In show jumping, riders complete a course of jumps with lots of twists and sharp turns in the fastest time possible without getting penalized for knocking any poles down.

Dressage is the horse ballet one, where horse and rider perform a pattern, sometimes to music. All that's missing are some disco lights. Judges award points for obedience, flexibility, and balance, and the highest score wins. Dressage also appears at the Paralympics.

Eventing is three different events on the same horse—dressage, show jumping, and cross-country. A cross-country course has natural obstacles like fallen trees, walls, water jumps, and hedges. The horse and rider with the lowest number of combined penalties win.

A BIT OF HISTORY
In the past, humans were very lazy and got bored of walking to places. Luckily, they managed to persuade horses to do all the work and even jump over things that got in their way, and so equestrian was born.

The ancient Games featured chariot racing, but in 1900, they ditched the chariot and stuck to jumping over fences instead.

Skills Needed
You need top-notch horse-riding skills. The rider must use the reins and their legs, shifting their body weight around to communicate with the horse. Talking to the horse isn't allowed in dressage, but that's okay because nobody really knows how to speak "horse" anyway.

JUMPING

JUMPING HELMET
Important to protect your noggin if you take a tumble

A FENCE
Horses aren't allowed to knock down any poles, stop in front of a jump, or run around it.

UPSIDES

Along with the modern pentathlon, it's the only sport in the Games where you have to control an animal. You can be any age—the second oldest Olympian ever, Austria's Arthur von Pongracz, was 72 when he competed in the 1936 Summer Games!

DOWNSIDES

It's dangerous. A horse deciding he has had enough of you on his back or falling on top of you can really hurt. It can get a bit smelly, too.

Sound Like a Pro

"TACK"
Equipment on a horse, including a saddle and a bridle

"PIROUETTE"
The horse turns 360 degrees by pivoting on the inside back leg

"NICKER" or **"WHICKER"**
A horse's soft whinny, used as a greeting to humans or other animals

"PIAFFE"
Dressage term for trotting in place

"REFUSAL"
When a horse stops at a jump

DRESSAGE

DRESSED UP
A helmet or top hat, tailcoat, white gloves, white breeches, and tall black boots. Spiffy!

BRAIDED MANE
In dressage, the horse needs to look immaculate with the mane neatly braided.

MUSIC
The horse is supposed to dance artfully to the music in the freestyle, or kür, so pick your tune wisely. Heavy metal probably wouldn't work!

BEST EVER:

Germany leads the pack with 52 medals, 25 of which are gold. Sweden is next, with 43 medals, 17 gold.

Germany's Isabell Werth is the most successful equestrian athlete ever, with ten medals, six of them gold.

Great Britain has a whopping 56 medals at the Paralympics, 31 gold. Lee Pearson has 14 medals, 11 gold.

PEARSON'S MEDAL COUNT:

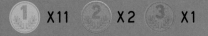

① X11   ② X2   ③ X1

CHANCE OF BECOMING A CHAMPION

Slim	Okay	Good	Great

Equestrian is not something you can just do in gym after math class. It is not a cheap sport, and riders usually own or have been around horses since they were very young.

SKATEBOARDING

WHAT IS IT?

Riding a small wooden board with four chunky wheels attached to the bottom while doing tricks and stunts

SKILLS NEEDED

Balance, skill, and courage. Learning all the tricks takes a lot of hard work, and some are dangerous, so if you get them wrong, it really hurts.

A BIT OF HISTORY

Skateboarding started in California in the 1950s when surfers decided to take their sport to the streets. It became huge in the 1980s and 1990s and finally reaches the Summer Games in 2020.

STAIRS

Usually boring things in houses that lead to bedrooms. In skateboarding you do tricks on them.

BASIC TRAINING

Throw yourself onto some cement over and over again. This will help you get used to falling off your board. Falling off is part of skateboarding, so pick yourself up and go again.

A CLOSER LOOK

RAMP

A perfect place to do slash grinds, fakies, blunt slides, bean plants, staple guns, and flyouts. Easy!

SKATEBOARD

The deck is usually made from layers of wood.

The Rules

There are two skate, or SK8 as some people call it, events at the Summer Games. In the "street" event, skaters show off their skills on a streetlike course that has stairs, benches, walls, slopes, curbs, and angry people shouting at them (okay, not that bit). The "park" event has deep and steep bowl-like ramps, which are perfect for performing high midair tricks.

Both events are scored by judges, who award points for difficulty and variety of tricks, quality of execution, speed, flow, and other aspects of skaters' runs.

CHANCE OF BECOMING A CHAMPION

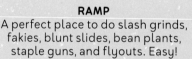

| Slim | Okay | Good | Great |

If you're still trying to master your first ollie, then you've got a long way to go. Only the cream of the crop gets to the Summer Games, and even then, there are currently only 80 slots for skateboarders, with a maximum of three from the same country in the same event.

BEST EVER

Skateboarding is new to the Summer Games, so time will tell who shines in this venue.

INJURIES

There isn't a skateboarder on earth who hasn't hurt themselves. If you're lucky, it will be a nasty bruise on the shin, some cuts, or a bit of road rash. If you're unlucky, you could break a bone, get concussed, or lose a tooth . . . or ten.

Sound Like a Pro

"DECK"
The board part of a skateboard

"STOKED"
Liking something a lot or being really excited

"OLLIE"
A trick in which, without using their hands, the skater gets their board to do a leap into the air

"NOSE SLIDE"
A slide on the front (nose) of the deck

"SKETCHY"
Used to describe anything that isn't good or trustworthy

"SLAM"
A really hard fall

SNEAKERS
Designed to be comfortable and hard-wearing

SKATEBOARDER FASHION
Includes baseball caps, beanies, hoodies, T-shirts, and baggy jeans or shorts

GRIND RAIL
Skaters use all parts of their board to slide along this rail.

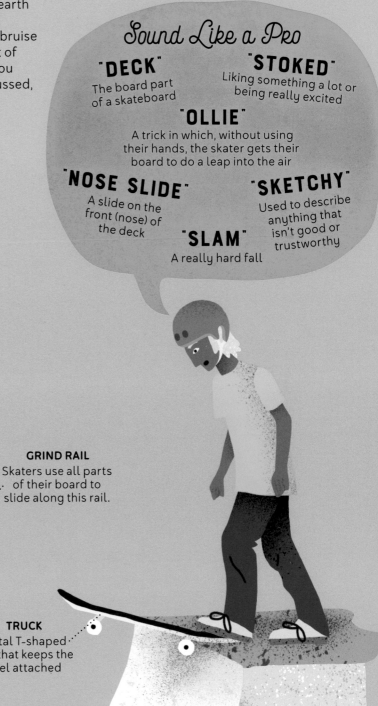

TRUCK
A metal T-shaped piece that keeps the wheel attached

UPSIDES

There's a great atmosphere at any skateboarding event, and the Summer Games have allowed DJs to play to help maintain that spirit. Events can be so much fun that the skateboarders may forget that they're supposed to be battling each other for a top spot.

DOWNSIDES

Banging your head on the curb after misjudging a trick does not look or feel good. Actually, banging any part of your body anywhere on a concrete surface hurts. If you're a bit of a moaner, stay away from skateboarding.

QUARTER-PIPE
A half-pipe is a U-shaped ramp with steep, sloping walls. A quarter-pipe is half a half-pipe.

WHAT ABOUT THE FUTURE?

New sports are popping up all the time. If enough people in enough countries start to play a new sport and it meets certain criteria set by the people in charge, then one day it, too, could be at the Summer Games. Here are just some sports that could be in the running.

TUG-OF-WAR

An old-school event: two teams try to pull a rope farther than their rivals.

Snooker & Billiards

In these sports, players use a stick, or cue, to knock different-colored balls into pockets at the sides and corners of a table covered in green material.

Kiteboarding

This is a water sport in which athletes ride the waves on a small wooden or foam board pulled along by a kite. The kites are more like the size of a parachute, not those tiny ones you take to the park.

NETBALL

A team ball sport, similar to basketball, but without dribbling or running with the ball. Players are given specific positions and are not allowed to stray outside certain areas of the court. It's arguably faster than basketball because of its three-second passing rule, which also encourages more teamwork.

AIR SPORTS

Potential new air sports include drone racing, gliding, parachuting, ballooning, aerobatics, and air racing.

BREAK DANCING

Break dancing looks set to feature in the 2024 Games, where B-boys and B-girls will perform street dance moves, including spins, pops, locks, freezes, windmills, and hand hops to music.

AMERICAN FOOTBALL

Confusingly called football even though most of the time players only use their hands. Heavily armored teams attempt to score touchdowns by running or throwing the ball into their opponents' end zone.

CHESS

Two players sit at a table moving pawns, knights, rooks, bishops, queens, and kings around a checkered board until someone gets something called checkmate. There's a long set of rules and it can get very complicated, so if you like watching two people silently staring at a board game for hours and hours, then this is the sport for you.

UNDERWATER SPORTS

Some potential new underwater sports include underwater hockey, soccer, and rugby; fin swimming; free diving; sport diving; and underwater wrestling, which is like regular wrestling but without the sweat.

Bowling

Bowling entails hurling a heavy ball down a lane to try to knock down ten pins and get a strike. Professional bowlers usually get a strike every time they bowl, and they also have their own bowling shoes, so they don't have to borrow those stinky ones you get at your local bowling alley.

WUSHU

A Chinese martial art in which athletes are judged on their fighting-style routines, which include kicks, punches, and jumps. Some people compare it to gymnastics, but the use of weapons such as swords, staffs, spears, and nunchucks gives it an edge.

FUTSAL

A bit like five-a-side soccer but played on a hard surface with a smaller, heavier ball that doesn't bounce very much.

ROLLER SPEED SKATING

This is a high-speed roller-skating race, a bit like speed skating but done on concrete rather than ice and with inline skates rather than ice skates. It's fast, frantic, and involves lots of crashes.

POLO

Polo has appeared at five modern Games and could make a comeback. Teams of four polo players ride horses, which they call ponies, and try to score goals by hitting a small hard ball through the rival team's goal using a long-handled mallet.

KARTING

Karting enthusiasts would like it to become the first motor sport at the Summer Games. Unlike in most professional motor sports, the karts are all the same, so it's a true test of the driver's skill.

ACROBATIC GYMNASTICS

A bit like very complicated cheerleading. Groups of gymnasts perform elegant moves, spins, twists, dances, and tumbles to music. It involves a high level of technical choreography and skill, as well as trust.

Squash

This is a very fast racket sport in which players thwack a small squidgy ball against some walls until their opponent can't hit it back anymore.

SUMO

An ancient Japanese type of wrestling in which two large men wearing massive belts called mawashi try to push each other outside a ring. Sumo is loaded with tradition, and wrestlers have a very strict way of life and training.

ULTIMATE FRISBEE

A mixed-team sport in which players score points by passing a plastic disc to a teammate in the opposing team's end zone. It's a long way from tossing a Frisbee on the beach for your dog to catch.

Glossary

APPARATUS — The term for equipment used by artistic gymnasts

ATHLETE — A person who is good at a sport; they are usually very fit and skilled

ATTACKER — A type of player on a team who tries to score goals or points

BATON — A short metal rod that athletes quickly hand to each other during a relay race

BOUT — The name for a match or a period of time in a combat sport

BULL'S-EYE — The center of a target

BUNKER — A big sand pit that traps golf balls

CARBON FIBER — A strong lightweight material made from carbon

CHALK — The white powder athletes use on their hands to help with their grip

CONCUSSION — When a whack on the head makes you feel strange or pass out

DEBUT — The first appearance

DEFENDER — A type of player who tries to stop the attacking players on the other team from scoring

DISQUALIFICATION — No more playing for you—bye-bye!

DRIBBLE — To move a ball forward by bouncing it—no saliva involved

FIBERGLASS — A lightweight material made from fine glass fibers

FLEET — A group of boats sailing together

FOUL — A prohibited move or play in a sport

GOALKEEPER or **GOALIE** — A player who protects the goal

HALF-PIPE — A U-shaped ramp used to perform tricks on

HORSE — An apparatus used in gymnastics—and the only Olympic animal

INJURY — Something that usually hurts and may mean you can't compete anymore

JUDGE — A person who awards marks or points in artistic or combat sports

KNOCKOUT — When a boxer punches their opponent and their opponent can't get up again

MARATHON — A very long race, around 42 kilometers (26 miles)

MAT — A soft floor covering that helps prevent athletes from hurting themselves when they land

MEDAL — A disk of gold, silver, or bronze that is hung around an athlete's neck if they come in first, second, or third

MIDDLE AGES — A long time ago when people didn't have the internet

NET — Strung between goalposts to stop a ball or across a court or table to provide a barrier in racket sports

OAR — A stick used to paddle a boat or canoe

OLYMPIC FLAME — A big torch that burns in the Olympic stadium during the Games

OLYMPIC GAMES — If you don't know about these by now, you haven't been paying attention.

OPPOSITION or **OPPONENT** — The rivals or rival in a competition

OUTFIELD PLAYER — In soccer: Any player who's not a goalkeeper. In baseball: A player positioned beyond the baselines.

PARALYMPIC GAMES — You really haven't been paying attention, have you?

PENALTY — The punishment for fouls; might take the form of points being deducted or the opposition getting a shot at the goal.

POOL — A large rectangle of water where swimmers compete

PROFESSIONAL — Someone who gets paid to do a job

PROSTHESES — Artificial body parts

RACKET — A kind of paddle with strings used in tennis and badminton

RALLY — A lot of back-and-forth shots in a court game, like tennis, badminton, or volleyball. A rally ends when a player fails to hit it back.

REFEREE — An official who keeps an eye on the rules and stops people from cheating

RELAY — A race in which each stage is run by a different member of a team

SAIL — A piece of material that helps power a boat

SPECTATOR — A person watching a sport, either live or on television

STAMINA — The energy inside you that keeps you going

STONE AGE — Even longer ago than the Middle Ages

SUBSTITUTE — A player who replaces another player when they are tired or playing badly

TACTICS — Special plans that help a team or an individual to reach their goal

TORCH RELAY — The Olympic flame is passed around the host country before being taken to the stadium to start the Games.

TOURNAMENT — A big competing event with a lot of athletes or teams

TRACK — An oval running area where athletes compete

UMPIRE — Another word for a referee

VICTORY — A win

VICTORY PODIUM — The special platform that an athlete stands on to receive their medal

WEIGHT CATEGORY — In many sports, athletes are weighed and placed in an appropriate category.

INDEX

Absalon, Julien 86
Adams, Nicola 35
Ainslie, Sir Ben 60
air sports 92
American football 92
ancient Egypt 22, 33, 58
ancient Greece 8, 20, 22, 34, 58, 69
ancient Rome 16, 29, 58
Andrianov, Nikolai 8
Angola 63
archery 32–33
athletics, decathlon 66–67
athletics, field events 64–65
  discus throw 65, 66, 67
  hammer throw 65
  high jump 64, 66
  javelin throw 65, 66, 67
  long jump 64, 66
  pole vault 64, 66, 67
  shot put 65, 66
  triple jump 64
athletics, heptathlon 66–67
athletics, track events 62–63
  hurdles 63, 66, 67
  long distance 63
  middle distance 63, 66, 67
  race walking 63
  sprinting 63, 66
Australia 9, 16, 17, 20
badminton 78–79
baseball 26–27
basketball 10–11
Belgium 9
billiards 93
boccia 22–23
Bolt, Usain 9, 63
bowling 93
boxing 34–35
Brazil 9, 13, 25
break dancing 92
Bulgaria 77
Canada 9, 15
canoe 54–55
chess 92
China 9, 12, 31, 33, 41, 45, 49, 77, 79, 83, 93
climbing, sport 72–73
Colombia 87
Coubertin, Baron Pierre de 8, 75
Cuba 27, 35, 44

cycling 74, 84–87
  BMX 87
  mountain bike 86
  road 84–85
  track 84–85
Cynisca of Sparta 8
Davydova, Anastasia 53
Deng Yaping 83
Denmark 15, 19
Dimas, Pyrros 77
diving 48–49
Egypt 22
England 22
equestrian 88–89
  dressage 88, 89
  eventing 88
  jumping 88, 89
Esajas, Wim 62
Felix, Allyson 63
fencing 36–37, 75
field events 64
Fiji 17
Finland 9, 15
Fischer, Birgit 9, 55
football 12–13
Fosbury, Dick 9, 64
France 8, 9, 19, 22, 37, 39, 40, 75, 80, 86
Frei, Heinz 8
Frisbee, ultimate 93
Fu Mingxia 49
futsal 93
Gao Ling 79
Germany 9, 18, 25, 37, 55, 59, 89
goalball 14–15
golf 28–29
Great Britain 9, 20, 28, 35, 50, 58, 59, 60, 78, 81, 82, 85, 89
Greece 9, 77
Guttmann, Dr. Ludwig 8
gymnastics, trampoline 70
gymnastics, acrobatic 93
gymnastics, artistic 68–69
gymnastics, rhythmic 71
handball 18–19
Hawaii 57
hockey 20–21
horse riding 75, 88–89
Hungary 13, 35, 37, 51, 55, 75
Hwang Kyung Seon 45

Icho, Kaori 42
India 20, 41, 78
Indonesia 79
Iran 25, 45
Ishchenko, Natalia 53
Italy 8, 9, 22, 37, 40, 86
Jamaica 63
Japan 9, 27, 38, 39, 40, 41, 42, 53, 68, 93
Jennings, Kerri Walsh 25
judo 38–39
Kahanamoku, Duke 57
karate 40–41
karting 93
Kenny, Laura 85
Kim Soo-nyung 33
kiteboarding 92
Latvia 87
Latynina, Larisa 8, 68
Leonidas of Rhodes 8
Lewis, Carl 9, 63
Lipă, Elisabeta 59
Lopez, Steven 45
Louganis, Greg 49
Mangiarotti, Edoardo 37
Marson, Roberto 8
Matos, Ángel 44
May-Treanor, Misty 25
Mexico 9
Milo of Croton 8
Mongolia 43
netball 92
Netherlands 9, 20
New Zealand 16
Nomura, Tadahiro 39
Osburn, Carl 31
Pajón, Mariana 87
Papp, László 35
Park, Inbee 28
Pearson, Lee 89
pentathlon, modern 75
Pezzo, Paola 86
Phelps, Michael 8, 9, 47, 68
Poland 77
polo 93
Portugal 23
Redgrave, Steve 9, 59
roller speed skating 93
Romania 9, 59
Romashina, Svetlana 53
rowing 58–59
rugby 16–17

running 62–63, 66, 67, 74, 75
Russia 11, 42, 53, 68, 71
Saei, Hadi 45
sailing 60–61
Savón, Félix 35
Sayovo, José 63
Scandinavia 18
Scotland 29, 65
Shields, Claressa 35
shooting 30–31, 75
skateboarding 90–91
snooker 92
softball 26–27
South Korea 9, 19, 23, 27, 28, 33, 45, 79, 83
Soviet Union 8, 9, 25, 68, 77
Spain 9, 40
squash 93
Stevenson, Teófilo 35
Štombergs, Māris 87
sumo 93
surfing 56–57
Sweden 9, 75, 89
swimming 46–47, 74, 75
swimming, artistic 52–53
Switzerland 8
table tennis 82–83
taekwondo 44–45
Tani, Ryoko 39
tennis 80–81
triathlon 74
tug of war 92
Turkey 42, 43
underwater sports 93
United Kingdom 9, 12, 16, 32
USA 8, 9, 10, 11, 13, 15, 17, 25, 27, 28, 31, 35, 42, 45, 47, 49, 51, 59, 63, 68, 74, 77, 81, 87, 90
USSR see Soviet Union
volleyball 24
Wang Nan 83
water polo 50–51
weightlifting 76–77
Werth, Isabell 89
Wiggins, Bradley 85
Williams, Serena 81
Williams, Venus 81
wrestling 42–43
wushu 93
Zorn, Trischa 8, 47